DEDICATION

*I dedicate this book, with love, to my mother and father,
Ruby and Norrell Ceaser*

Table of Contents

DISCLAIMER

ALTHOUGH I AM VERY CONFIDENT THAT YOU WILL OBTAIN THE DESIRED results, I must advise that, if you are under the care of a health care professional, any decision to stop using any medication or to discontinue counseling should be made in consultation with your medical and/or mental health care professional.

My Journey and What Led Me to Create These Affirmations

WHEN I STARTED MY JOURNEY to be a physician I would not have imagined that it would lead me to where I am today. My parents told me that I expressed a burning desire to become a doctor at the age of six. I wanted to help and heal people. It could be that my desire to become a medical doctor started with my love of watching Dr. Kildare and Dr. Marcus Welby on television. No matter the origin, my desire to be a healer persisted throughout my early years and I was determined to succeed.

I started the journey by attending a public elementary school in Chicago, Bryn Mawr Elementary, and later, South Shore High School. From there I traveled to the Ivy towers of Dartmouth College. Following my undergraduate studies, I returned to Chicago for medical school and residency at the University of Illinois. After my residency, I worked in an inner-city clinic and at the Cook County Correctional Facility, in order to fulfill my obligation with the National Health Service Corps.

Upon fulfilling my obligation, I started a private medical practice a few miles away from my childhood home. Initially the practice of medicine was both rewarding and challenging. I had daily opportunities to develop my diagnostic and treatment abilities. Additionally, my regular interactions with patients, and dealing with their physical, emotional and mental challenges, enabled me to grow as a person and as a physician. Eventually, however, I began to feel as if part of the equation was missing. I could diagnose their illnesses, prescribe the proper medication and provide advice on lifestyle changes for the purposes of alleviating their symptoms and controlling their ailments. Yes, I was helping, but rarely healing my patients.

I began to have second thoughts about how I was practicing medicine. I could not imagine that the father of medicine, to whom I took an oath, was content merely to manage diseases. Driven to acquire the knowledge to heal my patients as opposed to managing their ailments, I decided to venture out and explore the realm of alternative, non-Western, medicine. Alternative approaches to treating and curing diseases and physical conditions have been in existence for thousands of years. These approaches encompass a myriad of techniques, including the use of herbs, supplements, aromatherapy and physical manipulation. Evidence abounds that, prior to the evolution of modern medicine, the fathers of medicine used herbs and other modalities to heal the same diseases that we now treat or manage.

My newfound focus led me to a course on herbal supplements. I learned how to use muscle testing (kinesiology) to select the most appropriate vitamin and mineral supplements to address specific deficiencies within the human body. The same course included a session on how to change thought patterns and emotions using affirmations, tapping and muscle testing. There is substantial evidence suggesting one could reprogram thoughts, emotions or beliefs by repeating specific affirmations over a period of twenty-one days, along with tapping certain parts of the body. At that time, I had more than my fair share of stress, and I was in need of some reprogramming. Therefore, I spent hour after hour, day after day, tapping, repeating affirmations and muscle testing. I nearly tapped a hole in my head! I was able to obtain some results using these methods but not at the pace that I desired.

One night while reciting the affirmations, without tapping, but just focusing on an issue, I realized that my perspective on that issue had instantly changed in a positive way. Initially I had muscle tested that issue and it was weak. Afterwards when I muscle tested the issue it was strong. To assure myself that this was no fluke, I tried another issue and, similarly, there was an instant change. These results made me re-examine the prior experiences I had with my patients and muscle testing. Previously, when I performed muscle testing on patients with various supplements I would get inconsistent results. One moment a patient would test strong, the next moment the patient would test weak, all while using the same supplement. I realized that by changing my thoughts, I could affect the outcome of the muscle testing. If I wanted the patients to test strong they would test strong and if I wanted them to test weak they would test weak. I became aware that I could affect the thoughts and emotions of others (with their assistance) much in the same manner that I was able to change instantly my own thoughts and emotions.

With these discoveries, my journey took an unexpected turn. Every day for the next nine years, I spent literally four to twelve hours a day searching and exploring my inner self. My intention was to uproot every negative thought, belief, and emotion that resided within me and either eliminate it or change it to a positive. I would use various combinations of positive words and phrases in an attempt to make a permanent change. I used countless affirmations, targeting the Ego, the Subconscious Mind, the Conscious Mind, the Higher Self and others. I targeted anything within me that I thought would listen. After many years, I finally settled on targeting my "Inner Self". I did not know that when I started the journey that I would have to relive and suffer through my darkest hours. I experienced emotions of sadness, depression, hopelessness, helplessness and fear. I thought and felt things that I would never have imagined were a part of me.

During the course of my transformation, I experienced many highs and lows. I would walk in the dark, inside my home in Hyde Park/Kenwood, for countless hours trying to resolve intense emotional feelings or remove negative thoughts and impulses, not having an idea from where they originated. I suspected that my family thought that I was losing it. In fact, the opposite was happening; I was coming into a state of clarity. Fortunately, I undertook my journey, and although my journey is not complete, I have finally reached a level of success and satisfaction and I feel that I am on the right path.

Over the years, I have helped thousands of people overcome many problems, ranging from depression, suicidal thoughts, post-traumatic stress, phobias, low self-esteem, confidence issues, and various addictions. Fortunately, for them, when they repeat the affirmations the changes happen so quickly that they do not have to relive or experience any unwanted pain. Other than for someone who is completely out of touch with reality, I have not encountered a problem that I was not able to help or eliminate. I have been successful in helping people face to face, by telephone and through audio recordings and the use of written affirmations.

On numerous occasions, people have asked how it is that I can instantly make changes in thoughts, feelings and beliefs. Truthfully, I do not have a concrete explanation. I do know that when I have someone repeat an affirmation I can detect a subtle energy flowing through my body. When I stop repeating the affirmations, the energy flow ceases. The main challenge over the years was to find the right word and phrases that resonated with my inner self and made the appropriate change. I found that once I changed my inner self's thoughts, feelings or beliefs mine would also instantly change. I found that if the words resonated with my inner self it would resonate with anyone's inner self.

The affirmations in this book are for positive transformation. The intent of the affirmations is to make an instant and permanent change. If you decide to change the words, for whatever reason, chances are they will not work.

Within this book, I have included a variety of topics: depression, anxiety, recovering from sexual assault, correcting behavioral disorders, increasing confidence, improving self-esteem, affirmations for children and teenagers, affirmations for parents, weight loss, tobacco and alcohol cessation, and many others. I recommend that you use as many of the affirmations as possible, in order to address the inevitable internal resistance and denial. There will be no harm in repeating any of the affirmations.

The purpose of this book is to eliminate as much negative energy within you and within our society as possible. The purpose is to help those in need of emotional, physical, mental and spiritual relief. To use this book effectively, choose a topic, and then silently, in your mind, repeat the affirmation a minimum of three to five times, and move on to the next affirmation. You will become more relaxed and detect a shift in consciousness. Some have reported warm feelings throughout their bodies. The majority of people experience a feeling of lightness, as if a load has been lifted. Along with the physical sensations, you will also detect a positive change in how you perceive the problem that you were addressing or that it no longer exists.

If you desire, you can return to any of the affirmations as often as you like. The words of the affirmations are empowered so that you can read the affirmations to anyone and, when they repeat the affirmations as instructed, they will get the intended results. The affirmations can be read to any size group of people, all will get the intended results if they repeat the affirmations as instructed. You can even translate the affirmations into a different language for someone who does not speak English. I usually have people close their eyes while repeating the affirmations, to get into a more relaxed state, but it is not necessary.

I sincerely thank you for selecting and using this book. I am certain that you will find this book to be valuable and that it lives up to its name, **"The Most Powerful Book of Affirmations Ever Written"**. If you know of anyone who can be helped by this book please spread the word, for we are truly all in this together.

Dr. Sheldon T. Ceaser
April 26, 2013

INSTRUCTIONS ON PROPER USE OF THE AFFIRMATIONS

When using this book, choose an issue and repeat each of the listed affirmations. Repeat each silently to yourself, for a minimum of three to five times. Then move on to the next affirmation. If you desire, you can return to the affirmations as often as you like. If you are reading the affirmations to someone, have them repeat the affirmations silently, in their mind, three to five times. I usually have people close their eyes to get into a more relaxed state, but this is not necessary. As an example please repeat the following two affirmations to yourself three times:

MY INNER SELF IS ALWAYS POSITIVE.

MY INNER SELF BELIEVES THAT I SHOULD ALWAYS BE POSITIVE.

Overcoming Negative Emotional States

STRESS

1. My inner self never believes that anything is stressful for any reason.

2. My inner self is never stressed for any reason.

3. My inner self does not believe that I should feel stressed for any reason.

4. My inner self believes that it is always possible to be stress-free under any condition.

5. My inner self never feels that anything that I am doing is stressful for any reason.

6. My inner self never feels pressured for any reason.

7. My inner self is never stressed at work for any reason.

8. My inner self is never stressed by personal relationships for any reason.

9. My inner self is never stressed by family, friends or strangers for any reason.

10. My inner self is never stressed when competing.

11. My inner self is never stressed when attempting to meet a deadline.

12. My inner self is never stressed about finances.

13. My inner self is never stressed about money.

14. My inner self is never stressed when things do not go according to plans.

15. My inner self is not stressed by anything that happened in the past.

16. My inner self is not stressed by anything that is happening now.

17. My inner self is not stressed about anything that may happen in the future.

18. My inner self never feels overwhelmed for any reason.

19. I do not believe that my inner self should feel overwhelmed.

20. My inner self does not believe that I should ever feel overwhelmed.

21. My inner self never becomes frustrated for any reason.

22. My inner self never feels agitated for any reason.

23. My inner self does not believe that I should ever feel agitated for any reason.

24. My inner self is never stressed by natural calamities or disasters.

25. My inner self is never stressed about unfulfilled desires, unfulfilled wishes, unfulfilled needs or unfulfilled prayers.

26. My inner self never feels stressed for unknown reasons.

27. My inner self does not believe in doing harmful things to relieve stress.

28. My inner self is always able to calm its mind and relax under any condition.

29. My inner self believes that I should be able to calm my mind and relax under any condition.

30. My inner self never needs fear or stress to do what needs to be done.

31. I do not believe that I should feel tense for any reason.

32. My inner self never feels tense for any reason.

33. My inner self does not believe that I should feel tense for any reason.

34. My inner self does not believe that I should feel stressed for any reason.

ANXIETY AND PANIC DISORDERS

1. I do not believe that my inner self should panic under any condition for any reason.

2. My inner self never panics under any condition for any reason.

3. My inner self never feels like panicking for any reason.

4. My inner self never feels panicky.

5. My inner self does not panic and does not believe that I should ever panic for any reason.

6. My inner self does not believe that I should feel like panicking for any reason.

7. My inner self does not believe that I should ever feel panicky.

8. My inner self is not afraid of anything or anyone, and does not believe that I should feel afraid for any reason.

9. My inner self does not believe that there is anything to fear.

10. My inner self is not anxious about anything that happened in the past.

11. My inner self is not anxious about anything that may happen in the future.

12. My inner self never feels anxious for any reason.

13. My inner self does not feel anxious.

14. My inner self does not believe that I should feel anxious for any reason.

15. My inner self never feels anxious for unknown reasons.

16. My inner self never feels anxious about past, present or future events for any reason.

17. My inner self never feels anxious when under pressure or in stressful situations for any reason.

18. My inner self never feels anxious about what someone else is experiencing.

19. My inner self does not believe that I should ever feel anxious because of unfulfilled desires.

20. My inner self never feels anxious, nervous, tense or fearful for any reason.

21. My inner self does not believe that I should feel anxious.

22. My inner self does not believe that there are any reasons to be anxious.

23. My inner self believes that I should relax and be calm.

FEARS AND PHOBIAS

1. I do not believe that my inner self should fear anything.

2. My inner self never feels fear.

3. My inner self does not believe that I should fear anything for any reason.

4. I do not believe that my inner self should feel afraid for any reason.

5. My inner self does not believe that I should feel afraid for any reason.

6. My inner self never feels frightened for any reason.

7. I do not believe that my inner self should dread anything for any reason.

8. I do not believe that my inner self should react out of fear for any reason.

9. I do not believe that my inner self should feel terrorized for any reason.

10. My inner self is never terrified of anything for any reason.

11. I do not believe that my inner self should feel terrified for any reason.

12. My inner self never feels vulnerable for any reason.

13. My inner self never feels threatened for any reason.

14. My inner self is not afraid of being robbed.

15. My inner self is not frightened by anything or anyone for any reason.

16. My inner self never feels insecure for any reason.

17. My inner self never feels unsafe for any reason.

18. My inner self never feels apprehensive for any reason.

19. My inner self believes that I am able to conquer all of my fears.

20. I believe without a doubt that I am able to conquer all of my fears.

21. I want to conquer all of my fears.

22. My inner self will never fear death for any reason.

23. My inner self is not fearful of anything that happened in the past.

24. My inner self will never be fearful of what may happen in the future.

25. My inner self feels safe and secure and never feels unsafe for any reason.

26. My inner self does not believe that I should ever be afraid for any reason.

27. My inner self does not feel it will be harmed in any way.

28. My inner self never feels afraid that any harm will happen to my loved ones or me.

29. My inner self will never feel afraid of failing for any reason.

30. My inner self is never afraid of taking chances.

31. My inner self does not believe that I should be afraid of taking chances unless it is not worth the consequences.

32. My inner self never takes unnecessary chances or risks.

33. My inner self never feels afraid of making mistakes or messing up.

34. My inner self is never fearful of what people are thinking.

35. My inner self does not feel that it is ever all right for me to feel afraid for unknown reasons.

36. My inner self will never be afraid of the afterlife.

37. My inner self is not afraid of losing anything for any reason.

38. My inner self is not afraid of dying and leaving loved ones behind.

39. My inner self does not feel afraid.

40. My inner self does not feel afraid even in dangerous or life-threatening situations.

41. My inner self never needs fear to do what needs to be done.

42. My inner self never reacts out of fear for any reason.

43. My inner self does not believe that there is anything to fear.

44. My inner self believes that, without a doubt, all my fears have been overcome.

45. My inner self always feels brave.

46. My inner self believes that I should feel safe.

47. My inner self never feels claustrophobic for any reason.

48. My inner self does not think that I should feel afraid in enclosed, small spaces, for any reason.

49. My inner self does not believe that any harm will come to me when I am in enclosed spaces.

50. My inner self is not affected in small, enclosed spaces.

51. My inner self does not believe that I should be affected when in enclosed spaces.

52. My inner self is never fearful of performing in public.

53. My inner self does not believe that I should be fearful of performing in public.

54. My inner self never feels afraid of speaking in public for any reason.

55. My inner self does not believe that I should be fearful of speaking in public.

56. My inner self never feels afraid of flying for any reason.

57. My inner self does not believe that I should be afraid of flying.

58. My inner self never feels afraid of driving for any reason.

59. My inner self does not believe that I should be afraid of driving under any weather condition or at any normal speed.

60. My inner self never feels afraid of heights for any reason.

61. My inner self does not believe that I should be afraid of heights.

62. My inner self never feels afraid of snakes for any reason.

63. My inner self does not believe that I should be afraid of snakes.

64. My inner self is not afraid of mice or rats.

65. My inner self does not believe that I should be afraid of mice or rats.

66. My inner self does not believe that I should be afraid of clowns.

67. My inner self is fearless.

WORRY

1. My inner self does not believe that worrying will ever accomplish anything.

2. My inner self does not believe that I should worry about things that might happen for any reason.

3. My inner self does not believe that I should worry about myself for any reason.

4. My inner self does not believe that I should worry about anyone for any reason.

5. My inner self never worries about finances for any reason.

6. My inner self never worries for any reason.

7. My inner self does not believe that I should ever worry about my safety or anyone else's safety.

8. My inner self believes that I should always be careful and cautious, and never reckless.

9. My inner self never worries about what other people are thinking.

10. My inner self never worries about how people feel about me.

11. My inner self never worries about making mistakes.

12. My inner self never worries about failing for any reason.

13. My inner self does not think that I should ever worry about things that happened in the past for any reason.

14. My inner self does not believe that I should ever worry about anything that is happening now.

15. My inner self does not believe that I should ever worry about future events.

16. My inner self does not feel worried.

17. My inner self does not believe that I should feel worried for any reason.

18. My inner self believes that, without a doubt, one can always be worry-free.

19. My inner self believes that I should feel that everything is going to be all right.

SUICIDE

1. My inner self wants to be helped.

2. I believe that my inner self wants to be helped.

3. Nothing can make me want to end my life for any reason.

4. My inner self will never feel that I do not have a reason to live.

5. My inner self will never think or feel that nothing matters.

6. My inner self does not believe that anything is unbearable.

7. My inner self will never feel helpless for any reason.

8. I do not believe that I should ever harm myself in any way, for any reason.

9. My inner self does not believe that I should harm myself.

10. My inner self will never be self-destructive for any reason.

11. My inner self is not negatively affected by things that happened in the past for any reason.

12. My inner self feels that life is always worth living, no matter what I am going through.

13. My inner self always feels that its life is meaningful.

14. My inner self believes that I have a reason and a purpose to continue living.

15. My inner self believes that I should never feel, for any reason, that my life is not worth living.

16. My inner self never feels like giving up for any reason.

17. My inner self will never feel as if it cannot continue living for any reason.

18. My inner self does not feel that life is not worth living and never will feel that way for any reason.

19. My inner self will never be tired of living for any reason.

20. My inner self will never lose interest in living for any reason.

21. My inner self will never feel, for any reason, that life has no meaning.

22. My inner self always desires to live.

23. My inner self wants to live.

24. My inner self believes that I should want to live.

25. My inner self will never feel like committing suicide for any reason.

26. My inner self does not believe that I should ever feel like committing suicide for any reason.

27. My inner self does not want to die.

28. My inner self does not believe that I should ever feel like harming myself in any way.

29. My inner self always cares about living.

30. My inner self will never wish that it were dead for any reason.

31. My inner self does not believe that I should ever wish that I were dead for any reason.

32. My inner self does not believe that I should kill myself for any reason.

33. My inner self desires to live.

34. My inner self believes that I am able to recover completely from the incident leading up to my decision or desire to commit suicide.

35. My inner self no longer feels sad or depressed.

36. My inner self no longer feels that suicide is the solution to my problems.

37. My inner self will never believe that suicide is an option.

38. My inner self feels neutral to all bad memories and bad experiences.

39. My inner self believes I will find a way to survive and thrive.

40. My inner self never believes that all is lost.

41. My inner self always loves life.

42. My inner self loves me.

43. My inner self believes that I should love myself.

44. I love myself.

45. My inner self is no longer suffering.

46. My inner self is no longer in pain.

47. My inner self no longer hurts.

48. My inner self has always been resilient and adaptable and my inner self will adapt.

49. My inner self does not believe in committing suicide.

50. My inner self does not want me to commit suicide.

51. My inner self cares about living.

52. My inner self will always have the will to survive.

53. My inner self does not think or feel that my life is sad or depressing.

54. My inner self believes that I will find a way to adapt and overcome this present situation.

55. My inner self believes that I will find a way to be happy.

56. My inner self believes that it should always be happy.

57. My inner self believes that I should always be happy.

POST-TRAUMATIC STRESS DISORDER

1. My inner self is able to recover rapidly from any traumatic event.

2. My inner self does not feel traumatized.

3. I do not believe that my inner self should ever feel traumatized for any reason.

4. My inner self does not believe that I should ever feel traumatized.

5. I do not believe that my inner self should suffer for any reason.

6. My inner self is not suffering.

7. My inner self is not feeling any pain or hurt.

8. I do not believe that my inner self should feel pain or hurt for any reason.

9. I do not believe that my inner self should feel traumatized by anything that happened in the past for any reason.

10. I do not believe that my inner self should feel any pain or suffering related to the past for any reason.

11. My inner self feels completely recovered from all of my past negative experiences.

12. My inner self believes that I should feel completely recovered from all of my past negative experiences.

13. My inner self never feels upset when talking about traumatic events.

14. My inner self will always recover, quickly and completely, from any traumatic event.

15. My inner self feels completely neutral to all past traumatic events.

16. My inner self feels completely neutral to all bad memories and bad experiences.

17. My inner self is never affected by traumatic events that happened in the past for any reason.

18. My inner self is completely over all traumatic events.

19. My inner self's mind is never preoccupied with traumatic events.

20. My inner self is not angry or upset about any traumatic event.

21. My inner self is not sad or depressed and will not be sad or depressed for any reason.

22. My inner self does not feel victimized.

23. My inner self is strong and resilient.

24. My inner self truly wants to let go of the past and move on.

25. My inner self believes that I should let go of the past and move on.

26. My inner self believes that I should be able to talk about any traumatic experiences without them having a negative effect on me.

27. My inner self believes that I should be able to remember any traumatic experiences, if I desire, without them having a negative effect on me.

28. My inner self believes that I should forgive all those involved, in any way, in all traumatic events that I have experienced.

29. My inner self believes that I will find a way to adapt and overcome this present situation.

30. My inner self feels relieved.

31. My inner self believes that I should feel at peace with the past.

ANGER

1. My inner self cannot be irritated or angered by anyone or anything, for any reason.

2. My inner self does not believe that I should feel angry or upset for any reason.

3. My inner self can never be provoked for any reason.

4. I do not believe that my inner self should feel hostile for any reason.

5. My inner self never holds animosity towards anyone, for any reason.

6. My inner self will never feel like exploding for any reason.

7. My inner self is never violent or destructive for any reason.

8. My inner self never feels violent or destructive for any reason.

9. My inner self never feels combative for any reason.

10. My inner self will never desire to kill anyone or anything, for any reason.

11. My inner self does not believe that I should ever overreact for any reason.

12. My inner self does not believe that I should be angry with myself for any reason.

13. My inner self does not become upset for any reason.

14. I do not believe that my inner self should become upset for any reason.

15. My inner self is never bitter for any reason.

16. My inner self never loses control for any reason.

17. My inner self never feels mean for any reason.

18. My inner self never acts mean for any reason.

19. My inner self never feels confrontational for any reason.

20. My inner self never thinks about committing violent or destructive acts for any reason.

21. My inner self does not believe that I should ever lose control of my temper for any reason.

22. My inner self never feels angry for any reason.

23. My inner self does not believe that I should become angry for any reason.

24. My inner self does not believe that I should be angry.

25. My inner self does not believe that I should feel angry.

26. My inner self does not believe that I should ever lose control of my emotions for any reason.

27. My inner self believes in settling all disagreements without becoming angry.

28. My inner self never has angry thoughts.

29. My inner self does not believe that I should commit violent or destructive acts out of anger.

30. My inner self does not believe that I should ever harm anyone out of anger.

31. My inner self does not think that I should ever seek revenge out of anger.

32. My inner self does not think I should react angrily for any reason.

33. My inner self believes that any situation can be handled without becoming angry.

34. My inner self never thinks violent, destructive or harmful thoughts for any reasons.

35. My inner self does not think that I should ever harm myself out of anger.

36. My inner self is not angry about anything that happened in the past.

37. My inner self does not believe that I should be negatively affected if anyone talks to me in a way that I do not like.

38. My inner self does not believe that I should feel or think negatively for any reason.

39. My inner self does not become angry for any reason.

REGRETS AND RESENTMENTS

1. My inner self does not believe that I should feel any regrets about anything that happened in the past.

2. My inner self does not resent anyone or anything.

3. My inner self does not believe that I should ever feel resentful.

4. All regrets have been permanently eliminated.

5. All resentments have been permanently eliminated.

SADNESS AND DEPRESSION

1. My inner self never feels that anything is depressing for any reason.

2. My inner self does not feel sad or depressed, and will never feel sad or depressed for any reason.

3. My inner self believes that it is all right for me not to feel sad or depressed and to never feel sad or depressed for any reason.

4. My inner self does not believe that I should be sad or depressed because of present situations for any reason.

5. My inner self will never feel sad or depressed about anything that happened in the past for any reason.

6. My inner self never feels sad or depressed about any future event.

7. My inner self never feels sad or depressed because of the weather.

8. My inner self does not believe that I should feel sad or depressed because of the day of the week or the month of the year.

9. My inner self never feels sad or depressed because of financial issues.

10. My inner self does not feel sad or depressed without a companion.

11. My inner self does not feel sad or depressed when things end.

12. My inner self does not feel sad or depressed during departures.

13. My inner self does not feel sad or depressed when relationships end.

14. My inner self is always able to overcome the sadness and depression associated with the death of a loved one.

15. My inner self never feels that nothing matters.

16. My inner self never feels like crying unless it is tears of joy.

17. My inner self does not feel like crying.

18. My inner self will never lose interest in all things for any reason.

19. My inner self never feels detached for any reason.

20. My inner self believes that it should always be happy.

21. My inner self believes that I should be happy despite all that I have been through.

22. My inner self believes that I can be happy again.

REVENGE

1. My inner self does not believe that I should seek revenge for any reason.

2. My inner self does not believe that I should ever feel revengeful for any reason.

3. My inner self never feels like seeking revenge for any reason.

4. My inner self does not believe in being vindictive for any reason.

5. My inner self is not vindictive.

6. My inner self is always forgiving.

HATE

1. My inner self does not hate anyone or anything, for any reason.

2. My inner self will never hate anyone or anything, for any reason.

3. I do not believe that my inner self should hate anyone or anything, for any reason.

4. All traces of hate have been removed from my inner self.

5. I believe that all traces of hate have been removed from my inner self.

6. My inner self never has feelings of dislike or hate for anyone, for any reason.

7. My inner self does not believe that I should ever have feelings of dislike or hate for anyone, for any reason.

8. My inner self will always have a good heart that is filled with love and joy.

GRIEF

1. My inner self does not believe that anything is unbearable.

2. My inner self does not believe that I should grieve for a long period of time.

3. My inner self does not grieve.

4. My inner self can rapidly overcome any painful event.

5. My inner self will always comfort me during the times that I am grieving.

6. My inner self believes that I should be able to overcome rapidly any painful event.

BLAME

1. My inner self does not blame anyone for anything that happened in the past.

2. My inner self does not believe that I should blame anyone for anything.

3. My inner self does not believe that I should blame myself for anything that happened in the past.

4. My inner self is always forgiving.

SORROW AND PITY

1. My inner self does not need to feel sorrow or pity to help someone.

2. My inner self never wants anyone's pity.

3. My inner self never feels sorry or pity for anyone.

4. My inner self is always concerned, compassionate and caring.

5. My inner self is always motivated to help those in need.

6. My inner self believes that I should always be motivated to help those in need.

SUFFERING

1. My inner self does not believe that my loved ones who have made their transition ever want me to suffer because of their departure.

2. My inner self does not have negative thoughts or feelings about death.

3. My inner self does not see death as the end of one's journey, but as a continuation of the journey.

4. My inner self does not believe that I should have any negative thoughts or feelings when thinking about departed loved ones.

5. My inner self believes that I should only have pleasant thoughts and feelings when thinking about departed loved ones.

6. My inner self does not believe that I should become sad or depressed on the anniversary of a loved one's transition.

7. My inner self never suffers for any reason.

8. My inner self does not want to suffer for any reason.

9. My inner self does not want me to suffer for any reason.

10. My inner self does not believe that I should suffer for any reason.

11. I am no longer suffering.

OBSESSIVE-COMPULSIVE BEHAVIOR

1. My inner self does not believe that I should be obsessive-compulsive for any reason.

2. My inner self never believes that I always have to do things a certain way.

3. My inner self is always open to changing the way that things are done.

4. My inner self does not believe that I must follow the same routine every day or that I should be opposed to changing.

5. My inner self is not obsessive or compulsive.

6. My inner self is never negatively affected if things are not done a certain way.

7. My inner self does not believe that I should be affected if things are not done a certain way.

8. My inner self is never negatively affected if things are not in a certain order.

9. My inner self does not believe that I should be affected if things are not done in a certain order.

10. My inner self never has uncontrollable negative impulses.

11. My inner self does not believe that I should ever have uncontrollable negative impulses.

MENTAL INSTABILITY

1. My inner self never feels as if it is losing control of its mind for any reason.

2. My inner self will never feel disinterested in all things for any reason.

3. My inner self always thinks rationally.

4. My inner self never thinks irrationally for any reason.

5. My inner self does not believe that I should feel that the whole world is against me.

6. I do not believe that my inner self should become delusional for any reason.

7. My inner self is not delusional.

8. My inner self will never feel delusional.

9. I do not believe that my inner self should ever go insane for any reason.

10. My inner self is not insane.

11. I do not feel as if I am losing my mind.

12. I do not believe that my inner self should be overly possessive for any reason.

13. I do not believe that my inner self should feel paranoid for any reason.

14. My inner self does not believe that I should feel paranoid.

15. My inner self is not paranoid.

16. My inner self does not feel that anyone is coming to harm me.

17. My inner self does not feel that the whole world is plotting against me.

18. My inner self is not suspicious of everyone.

19. My inner self does not believe that I should be suspicious of everyone.

20. My inner self never distrusts everyone.

21. My inner self does not believe that anything within me should try to force me to do negative things against my will for any reason.

22. My inner self does not believe that I should hear negative internal voices at any time.

23. My inner self believes that all internal voices should be positive.

24. My inner self never feels as if it is losing its mind.

25. My inner self does not believe that I should ever feel as if I am going crazy.

26. My inner self does not believe that I should ever feel that I am about to have a nervous breakdown.

27. My inner self does not believe that everyone is against it and will never believe it for any reason.

28. My inner self does not believe that everyone is jealous of it.

29. My inner self never feels cold or callous for any reason.

30. My inner self will never feel out of touch with reality for any reason.

31. My inner self will never feel as if negative forces, whether internal or external, are controlling it.

32. My inner self is never negative, evil or sinister.

33. My inner self never feels negative, evil or sinister.

34. My inner self does not believe that I should feel or think negatively for any reason.

35. My inner self does not have another personality that is negative.

36. My inner self always feels good and positive.

DOUBTS

1. My inner self never doubts its abilities.

2. My inner self never doubts itself.

3. My inner self does not believe that I should doubt myself.

4. My inner self does not believe that I should ever doubt my abilities.

5. My inner self never doubts that all things are possible.

6. My inner self will never let doubts, whether mine or those of others, negatively influence me in any way.

7. My inner self does not believe that I should ever doubt myself for any reason.

REMORSE

1. My inner self always feels remorse when I do something that is not right.

2. My inner self believes that I should always feel remorseful when I do something that is not right.

FALSE PRIDE

1. My inner self is never too proud to admit when it is wrong.

2. My inner self is never too proud to apologize for any reason.

3. My inner self is never too proud to ask for help.

4. My inner self's pride will never be negatively affected by anyone for any reason.

5. I will not let my pride negatively affect me in anyway.

PROCRASTINATION

1. I do not believe that my inner self should ever delay doing things that need to be done now for any reason.

2. My inner self never delays in doing things that need to be done now.

3. My inner self does not believe that I should delay in doing things that need to be done now.

4. My inner self does not procrastinate.

5. My inner self does not believe that I should procrastinate for any reason.

6. My inner self does not believe that I should make excuses for not doing things that need to be done now.

7. My inner self never wants to wait until the last minute to do anything for any reason.

8. My inner self is always in the right state of mind to do what needs to be done now.

9. My inner self believes that I should always feel like doing what needs to be done.

EXCUSES

1. My inner self never makes excuses for any reason.

2. My inner self does not believe that I should make excuses.

3. My inner self does not believe that I should ever make excuses for not doing what needs to be done.

4. My inner self believes that I should always take personal responsibility for my actions.

CHAPTER 2

Enhancing and Creating Positive Emotional and Mental States

MOTIVATION

1. My inner self does not believe that I should ever be unmotivated for any reason.

2. My inner self always motivates and encourages me to do what needs to be done.

3. My inner self will always find a way to motivate me to do what I need to do.

4. My inner self is never unmotivated.

5. My inner self never feels unmotivated for any reason.

6. My inner self does not believe that I should ever feel unmotivated for any reason.

7. My inner self feels motivated to do all the things that need to be done today.

8. My inner self feels motivated to do all the things I want to do today.

9. My inner self believes that I should always feel like doing everything that needs to be done.

10. My inner self believes that I should always function at my best, even under adverse conditions.

11. My inner self always has the courage to do anything.

12. My inner self is always motivated to work extremely hard to obtain that which I desire.

13. My inner self feels motivated to do the things that need to be done.

14. My inner self is motivated to improve my present situation.

15. My inner self is always motivated to be successful.

16. My inner self is always motivated to be prosperous.

17. My inner self is always motivated to put forth the effort to accomplish my goals.

18. My inner self is always motivated to help others.

19. My inner self is always motivated to do good things.

20. My inner self is always motivated to be protective.

21. My inner self is always motivated to look out for others' well-being.

22. My inner self is always motivated to excel at any undertaking.

23. My inner self is always motivated to be happy and healthy.

24. My inner self is always motivated to learn new things.

25. My inner self is always motivated to develop new skills.

26. My inner self is always motivated to be productive.

27. My inner self is always motivated to be the best it can possibly be.

28. My inner self believes that I should always be motivated to do my best and be the best that I can possibly be.

29. My inner self never feels stagnated.

30. I do not believe that my inner self should ever feel stagnated.

31. My inner self does not believe that I should ever feel stagnated.

32. My inner self always feels motivated.

CONFIDENCE

1. My inner self is always confident and its confidence cannot be negatively affected by anyone or anything, for any reason.

2. My inner self will never feel as if it is incapable of doing anything, for any reason.

3. My inner self does not believe that there is anything wrong with my confidence.

4. My inner self believes that I should always feel confident.

5. My inner self believes that I should always be able to imagine myself confidently doing anything.

6. My inner self never lacks confidence in anything.

7. My inner self always has the courage to do anything.

8. My inner self always feels confident about everything.

9. My inner self believes that I should always be confident in my abilities and myself.

10. My inner self believes that I should always think and act confidently.

11. My inner self believes that I should always walk, talk and act confidently.

12. My inner self always feels confident.

13. My inner self believes that it is all right for me always to feel confident.

14. My inner self feels confident that it can excel at anything.

15. My inner self feels confident that it can succeed at anything.

16. My inner self feels that it can do all things just as good, if not better, than anyone else can do them.

17. My inner self feels confident in doing things that it has never done before.

18. My inner self believes that I should feel confident in doing things that I have not done before.

19. My inner self always feels confident about making the right decisions.

20. My inner self always feels confident that things will work out according to plans and expectations.

21. My inner self feels confident that I will be successful.

22. My inner self's confidence is never negatively affected by past events.

23. My inner self believes that I should feel confident that I could do anything.

SELF-ESTEEM

1. I do not believe that anything can ever demoralize my inner self.

2. My inner self never feels demoralized for any reason.

3. My inner self does not believe that I should ever feel demoralized.

4. My inner self never feels ashamed about anything that happened in the past.

5. I do not believe that my inner self should feel ashamed of anything that happened in the past for any reason.

6. I do not believe that my inner self should feel embarrassed about anything that happened in the past for any reason.

7. My inner self does not feel ashamed and will never feel ashamed for any reason.

8. My inner self does not feel embarrassed and will never feel embarrassed for any reason.

9. My inner self does not believe that I should ever feel ashamed or embarrassed for any reason.

10. My inner self does not feel traumatized and will never feel traumatized for any reason.

11. My inner self will never have a low self-esteem for any reason.

12. My inner self's self-esteem will always be high.

13. My inner self never feels insecure for any reason.

14. My inner self does not believe that I should ever allow myself to be taken advantage of, for any reason.

15. My inner self always feels wanted.

16. My inner self never feels unwanted for any reason.

17. My inner self always believes I should feel gifted.

18. My inner self never feels out of place for any reason.

19. My inner self never feels as if it does not belong for any reason.

20. My inner self never feels inferior to anyone for any reason.

21. My inner self never feels inferior for any reason.

22. My inner self believes that I should feel good about my appearance.

23. My inner self always feels good about itself.

24. My inner self never feels inadequate for any reason.

25. My inner self believes that I should always feel good about myself with or without a companion.

26. My inner self never feels rejected for any reason.

27. My inner self always feels proud.

28. My inner self believes that I should always feel proud.

29. My inner self does not believe that other people's opinion of me should ever affect me in a negative way.

30. Other people's opinions never have a negative effect on my inner self for any reason.

31. I do not believe that I should ever have a low opinion of myself for any reason.

32. My inner self never feels at a disadvantage for any reason.

33. My inner self always feels special.

34. My inner self believes that I should always feel special.

35. My inner self will never lose its dignity or self-respect for any reason.

36. My inner self will not be manipulated by anyone for any reason.

37. My inner self does not believe that I should dislike any part of my body for any reason.

38. My inner self does not believe that I should compare myself to anyone for any reason.

39. My inner self never feels that anyone is better than it is.

40. My inner self does not believe that I should ever wish that I were someone else.

41. My inner self does not believe that I should ever think that anyone is better than I am for any reason.

42. My inner self does not believe that I should ever feel disappointed in myself for any reason.

43. My inner self does not need approval from others to feel good.

44. My inner self never feels rejected for any reason.

45. My inner self believes that I should always feel good about myself.

46. My inner self never feels inadequate for any reason.

47. My inner self is not shy and does not believe I should be shy for any reason.

48. My inner self is never passive.

49. My inner self always feels invincible.

50. My inner self always feels beautiful.

51. My inner self thinks that I am beautiful.

52. I believe that I am beautiful.

FORGIVENESS

1. My inner self is always forgiving.

2. My inner self believes in completely forgiving everyone of everything all the time.

3. My inner self is not selective in forgiving.

4. My inner self believes that it has been completely forgiven of all things.

5. I believe that I have been completely forgiven of all things.

6. My inner self never holds a grudge for any reason.

7. My inner self never feels resentful for any reason.

8. My inner self never feels vindictive for any reason.

9. My inner self does not believe that I should have bad feelings for anyone.

10. My inner self does not blame anyone for anything that happened in the past.

11. My inner self does not treat the ones that were forgiven in a negative way.

12. Those who have been completely forgiven do not negatively affect my inner self.

13. My inner self never wishes harm to happen to anyone for any reason.

14. If desired, my inner self believes that it is acceptable to have normal relationships with those who have been completely forgiven.

15. My inner self is never preoccupied with, or dwells on, bad things that happened in the past.

16. If desired, my inner self believes that it is all right to forget about the harm or wrong that was done to me.

17. My inner self believes that, if I desire, I can feel the same way now as I did about the person(s) before the incident for which I have forgiven them.

18. My inner self believes that it is all right, if I desire, to treat the person(s) the same way as I did before the incident for which I have forgiven them.

19. My inner self believes in giving deserving people a second chance.

20. My inner self never has a problem accepting genuine apologies.

21. My inner self does not believe that I should ever have a problem forgiving.

CONCENTRATION

1. My inner self is able to focus and concentrate for any length of time.

2. My inner self believes that I should be able to focus and concentrate for any length of time.

3. My inner self is always able to focus and concentrate on one thing at a time.

4. My inner self believes that I should be able to focus and concentrate on one thing at a time.

5. My inner self is able to focus and concentrate under any condition.

6. My inner self believes that I should be able to focus and concentrate under any condition.

7. My inner self's mind is never preoccupied with something else when it should be focusing and concentrating on a particular subject or task.

8. My mind is not preoccupied with other things while I am focusing and concentrating on a particular subject or task.

9. My inner self is able to focus and concentrate without being distracted.

10. My inner self is never easily distracted for any reason.

11. My inner self does not believe that I should ever be easily distracted.

12. My inner self believes that I should always feel like doing what needs to be done.

13. My inner self believes that I should be focused on what I am doing and eliminate all unnecessary thoughts.

14. My inner self does not believe that I should have a problem focusing and concentrating for any reason.

RELAXATION

1. I believe that my inner self is able to relax under any condition.

2. My inner self believes that I should be able to calm down and relax under any condition.

3. My inner self does not believe that I should have a problem relaxing.

4. My inner self never has a problem calming down and relaxing.

5. My inner self feels calm and relaxed.

6. My inner self believes that I should feel calm and relaxed.

7. I feel calm and relaxed.

HAPPINESS, JOY AND FEELING GOOD

1. I believe that my inner self should always be able to be happy.

2. My inner self believes that it should always be happy.

3. Despite all that I have been through, my inner self believes that I should be happy.

4. My inner self believes it was born to be happy.

5. My inner self does not believe that I need a reason to be happy.

6. My inner self believes that I should be able to find joy in everything positive that I do.

7. My inner self always enjoys the company of others.

8. My inner self believes that everyone deserves to be happy and joyful at all times.

9. My inner self faces every new day with joy, happiness and hope.

10. My inner self believes that all joy and happiness comes from within.

11. My inner self always feels excited and enthusiastic about life.

12. My inner self always enjoys helping people.

13. My inner self enjoys having fun.

14. My inner self is full of life.

15. My inner self feels that everything is going to be all right.

16. My inner self feels whole and complete.

17. My inner self feels happy even under adverse conditions.

18. My inners self feels happy during good times and bad times.

19. My inner self feels happy going to work.

20. My inner self feels happy while at work.

21. My inner self feels happy during the holidays.

22. My inner self feels happy during the winter months.

23. My inner self feels happy on Mondays

24. My inner self feels happy when alone.

25. My inner self feels happy thinking about good memories.

26. My inner self feels happy thinking about future plans.

27. My inner self believes that I should be just as happy as it is.

28. My inner self feels dynamic.

29. My inner self feels inspired.

30. My inner self feels enthusiastic and excited.

31. My inner self always feels good when around family members.

32. My inner self always feels good when around friends and loved ones.

33. My inner self always feels good when around children.

34. My inner self always feels good even when around my least favorite people.

35. My inner self feels good helping people.

36. My inner self feels that it is wonderful to be alive.

37. My inner self feels powerful and in control.

38. My inner self believes that I should feel just as good as it does.

39. My inner self feels as if something good is about to happen.

40. My inner self feels loved and appreciated.

41. My inner self feels invincible.

42. My inner self feels lively.

43. My inner self feels like doing something good.

44. My inner self feels playful.

45. My inner self believes that I should always feel happy.

46. My inner self believes that I should always feel good.

INNER PEACE

1. I do not believe that anything should be able to interfere with my inner self's peace and serenity.

2. My inner self believes that I should feel peaceful and serene.

3. My inner self feels perfectly balanced.

4. My inner self believes that I should feel perfectly balanced.

5. My inner self feels peaceful and serene.

LOVE

1. I truly believe that my inner self loves me and will not stop loving me for any reason.

2. I love myself and I will not stop loving myself for any reason.

3. My inner self's heart is always filled with love and compassion.

4. My inner self always feels loved.

5. My inner self believes that I should always feel loved.

6. My inner self believes that I should love myself.

7. My inner self loves everyone.

8. My inner self believes that I should love everyone.

9. It is important to my inner self to love and to help others.

CHAPTER 3

Character Development

EMOTIONS

1. My inner self will never be obsessed over anything or anyone, for any reason.

2. I do not believe that anything or anyone can negatively affect my inner self's emotions.

3. My inner self believes that I should always have complete control of my emotions.

4. My inner self is affectionate and caring.

5. My inner self never has difficulty expressing its emotions for any reason.

6. My inner self does not believe that I should ever have a problem expressing my emotions.

7. My inner self never believes in negatively controlling people by manipulating their emotions.

8. My inner self always feels comfortable expressing all emotions.

9. My inner self is always in complete control of its emotions and feelings.

10. My inner self believes that I should always be in complete control of my emotions and feelings.

11. My inner self is never negatively affected by other people's emotions for any reason.

12. My inner self is not against having positive emotions and feelings for any reason.

13. My inner self will never be against having positive emotions and feelings for any reason.

CREATIVITY

1. My inner self is creative.

2. My inner self never has difficulty coming up with creative ideas.

3. My inner self can easily create anything.

4. My inner self enjoys being creative.

5. My inner self believes that I should always be able to come up with creative ideas when I need them.

6. My inner self always sends me creative ideas when I need them.

PATIENCE

1. My inner self is never impatient for any reason.

2. My inner self never minds waiting for any reason.

3. My inner self does not believe that I should be impatient for any reason.

4. My inner self does not believe that I should feel hurried.

5. My inner self does not believe that I should feel rushed.

6. My inner self does not believe that I should rush others.

7. My inner self does not believe that I should become restless or irritated while waiting.

8. My inner self does not believe that I should become angry while waiting.

9. My inner self does not believe that I should be angry or upset when someone is going slower than I want him or her to go.

10. My inner self is always tolerant.

11. My inner self is always patient and understanding.

12. My inner self believes that I should always be patient and understanding.

DEALING WITH THE PAST

1. My inner self is never negatively affected by bad memories for any reason.

2. My inner self does not blame anyone for anything that happened in the past.

3. My inner self does not believe that I should blame anyone for anything.

4. My inner self is not negatively affected by anything that happened in the past for any reason.

5. My inner self does not think that I should repeat the mistakes that I made in the past for any reason.

6. My inner self will never repeat the mistakes made in the past.

7. My inner self believes that I should be completely over all past bad experiences.

8. My inner self is completely over all past bad experiences.

9. My inner self believes that I should feel that I am completely over all bad experiences.

10. My inner self feels completely over all bad experiences.

11. My inner self believes that I should always be able to think of anything that happened in the past without it having a negative effect on me.

12. My inner self does not believe that I should feel that I am being punished for anything that happened in the past.

13. My inner self does not believe in thinking about bad experiences unless it is beneficial in some way.

14. My inner self never suffers from anything that happened in the past for any reason.

15. My inner self never feels upset when talking about anything that happened in the past.

16. My inner self does not believe that the past should negatively affect my future expectations.

17. My inner self does not believe that my past experiences should negatively influence the way that I think, feel, believe or act for any reason.

18. My inner self never dwells on, or thinks about, the pain and suffering that it endured in the past.

19. My inner self is completely over all bad things that happened in the past.

20. My inner self believes that I should always remember lessons learned from past experiences.

21. My inner self is at peace with the past.

DEALING WITH DISAPPOINTMENTS

1. I do not believe that my inner self should feel disappointed for any reason.

2. My inner self never feels disappointed for any reason.

3. My inner self does not believe that I should feel disappointed for any reason.

4. My inner self is never disappointed about anything that happened in the past for any reason.

5. My inner self is never affected by disappointments.

6. My inner self does not believe that I should be negatively affected when things do not happen the way that I want them to happen.

7. My inner self does not believe that I should be negatively affected if I do not get what I want.

MOOD AND DISPOSITION

1. My inner self's mood cannot be negatively affected by anyone or anything, for any reason.

2. My inner self's mood is never affected by other people's mood for any reason.

3. My inner self's mood and disposition are always positive.

4. My inner self does not believe that I should be in a negative mood for any reason.

5. My inner self is always in the mood to do all the things that need to be done.

6. My inner self believes that I should always be in the mood to do all the things that need to be done.

7. My inner self is not moody.

8. My inner self never makes excuses for being in a negative mood.

9. My inner self's mood is not unpredictable.

10. My inner self wants to be in a positive mood at all times.

11. My inner self believes that I should be in a positive mood at all times.

CARING

1. I believe that my inner self cares.

2. I do not believe that my inner self should stop caring for any reason.

3. My inner self never feels as if it does not care about anything for any reason.

4. My inner self always cares about living.

5. My inner self always cares about my well-being.

6. My inner self always cares about others.

7. My inner self always cares about the environment.

8. My inner self never feels as if it does not care about anyone.

9. My inner self always cares about every aspect of my life.

10. My inner self will never stop caring for any reason.

11. My inner self always cares about self-development.

12. My inner self believes that I should care as it does.

13. My inner self does not believe that I should stop caring about the things that I should care about.

STATE OF MIND

1. My inner self's state of mind cannot be negatively affected by anyone or anything, for any reason.

2. My inner self never feels out of touch.

3. My inner self never feels as if it is in a trance.

4. My inner self always feels emotionally and mentally balanced.

5. My inner self's state of mind is always positive.

6. My inner self never feels confused about anything, for any reason.

7. My inner self always feels mentally and emotionally prepared for anything that could possibly happen.

DESIRES

1. My inner self's desires cannot be negatively affected by anyone or anything, for any reason.

2. My inner self will never be controlled by any desires for any reason.

3. My inner self is always able to control its sexual desires.

4. All of my inner self's desires are associated with positive thoughts and feelings.

5. My inner self can always control its desire for anything.

6. My inner self will never feel as if it does not have any desires.

7. My inner self only desires positive things.

8. My inner self only desires to do positive things.

CHAPTER 4

Sexual Issues

RECOVERING FROM SEXUAL ABUSE/ASSAULT

1. I do not believe that my inner self should feel abused for any reason.

2. My inner self does not feel abused.

3. My inner self does not believe that I should feel abused.

4. I do not feel abused.

5. My inner self does not believe that other people's thoughts, feelings, emotions, words and actions should affect me in a negative way, for any reason.

6. My inner self does not believe that I should feel affected by past sexual assault.

7. My inner self does not believe that I should feel affected in any way by the sexual assault that I suffered.

8. My inner self does not believe that I should feel embarrassed or ashamed.

9. My inner self does not believe that I should feel violated.

10. My inner self does not believe that I should ever feel unclean related to the incident(s).

11. My inner self does not feel traumatized and will not feel traumatized for any reason.

12. My inner self does not believe that I should feel traumatized.

13. Thoughts of the sexual assault will no longer, and will not for any reason, have a negative effect on my inner self.

14. Thoughts of the sexual assault no longer affect me in a negative way.

15. My inner self is not angry over the assault.

16. My inner self does not believe that I should be angry.

17. My inner self never harbors any resentment or ill feelings towards anyone involved in the incident(s) for any reason.

18. My inner self does not believe that I should have any resentments or ill feelings towards anyone involved in the incident(s).

19. My inner self believes in forgiving.

20. My inner self forgives all those involved in my sexual assault.

21. My inner self believes that I should forgive all those involved in my sexual assault.

22. My inner self no longer thinks about the assault.

23. My inner self believes that I should be able to talk about the assault without being affected in any way.

24. My inner self does not feel that I am to blame for the assault.

25. I do not believe that I am to blame for the assault.

26. My inner self does not feel afraid of my attacker(s).

27. My inner self does not believe that I should feel afraid of my attacker(s).

28. My inner self will never be afraid to report the attack(s) for any reason.

29. My inner self believes that I should report the attack(s) to someone.

30. My inner self does not believe that the sexual assault should ever interfere with my ability to be intimate.

31. My inner self does not believe that I should think about the attack when I am being intimate.

32. My inner self does not believe that I should fear being sexually assaulted again.

33. My inner self does not believe that I should allow anyone to sexually assault me for any reason.

34. My inner self does not believe that I should think that I am going to be sexually assaulted again.

35. My inner self feels completely recovered from the assault.

36. My inner self believes that I should feel completely recovered.

CONTROLLING SEXUAL DESIRES

1. My inner self's sexual desires are never out of control for any reason.

2. My inner self is always able to control its sexual desires.

3. My inner self believes that I should always be able to control my sexual desires.

4. My inner self does not feel sexually frustrated and will never feel sexually frustrated for any reason.

5. My inner self does not believe that I should feel sexually frustrated.

6. My inner self does not believe in having nonconsensual sex for any reason.

7. My inner self does not believe in using sex to release stress or frustration for any reason.

8. My inner self can never be controlled by sex at any time for any reason.

9. My inner self does not believe that I should ever be controlled by sex.

10. My inner self never lusts for any reason.

11. My inner self does not always think about sex.

12. My inner self does not believe that I should always think about sex.

13. My inner self never suffers, for any reason, because of lack of sexual activity.

14. My inner self does not believe that I should ever suffer because of lack of sexual activity.

15. My inner self does not believe that I should be affected if I do not satisfy my sexual desires.

16. My inner self is never preoccupied with sex.

17. My inner self is in control of all its sexual desires.

18. Sexual desires will never interfere with my inner self's judgment at any time for any reason.

19. Sexual desires will never affect my inner self's thought process.

20. My inner self is never negatively influenced by sexual images.

21. My inner self never feels frustrated when it is not able to have sex.

22. My inner self's sexuality and ability to be intimate will never be affected by anything that happened in the past.

23. My inner self never desires or wants to sexually harm anyone in any way, for any reason.

24. My inner self believes that one can be sexually satisfied with one companion.

25. My inner self never yields to inappropriate sexual temptations for any reason.

26. My inner self never feels overwhelmed by sexual desires.

27. My inner self never feels that it has to have sex.

28. My inner self never suffers without having sex.

29. My inner self does not believe that I should suffer without having sex.

30. My inner self does not believe that I should feel that I have to have sex at this moment.

31. My inner self is not negatively affected, for any reason, when it cannot have sex at the time that it wants to have sex.

32. My inner self does not believe that I should be negatively affected when I cannot have sex when I want to have sex.

33. My inner self is never negatively affected if sexual advances are rejected.

34. My inner self's sexual desires are always associated with positive emotions, feelings and thoughts.

35. My inner self does not believe that I should ever have a problem saying "no" to sexual advances.

36. My inner self does not believe that I should feel bad saying "no" to any sexual advances.

37. My inner self does not believe that I should ever give in to pressure to have sex when I do not think that I should.

38. My inner self does not believe that I should feel tempted to do anything that I should not do.

39. All unwanted sexual desires and attractions have been eliminated from my inner self.

40. My inner self does not have any unwanted sexual desires or attractions.

41. My inner self does not believe that I should have any unwanted sexual desires or attractions.

42. My inner self does not feel sexually attracted to anyone whom, or to anything that, it does not want to have a sexual attraction.

43. My inner self does not believe that I should feel sexually attracted to anyone or anything for which I do not want to have a sexual attraction.

44. My inner self does not have any sexual desires for anyone whom, or for anything that, it does not want to have.

45. My inner self does not believe that I should have any sexual desires for anyone or anything that I do not want to have, or that I do not think that I should have.

46. My inner self cannot be influenced to be sexually attracted to anyone or anything for which it does not want to have a sexual attraction.

47. My inner self does not believe that I should perform any sex act that I do not want to perform for any reason.

48. My inner self does not believe that I should perform any sex act because everyone is doing it.

49. My inner self does not believe that I should ever feel pressured to perform any sexual act that I do not feel, believe or think is right.

50. My inner self does not believe that I should do anything to harm or degrade myself while engaging in sexual activities.

51. My inner self does not believe that I should do anything to harm or degrade anyone while engaging in sexual activities.

52. My inner self does not believe that I should ever get pleasure from pain for any reason.

53. My inner self does not desire to engage in any sexual activity that it does not believe, feel or think is right.

54. My inner self does not believe that I should ever sexually exploit anyone.

55. My inner self does not believe that I should ever allow myself to be sexually exploited.

56. My inner self does not believe that I should ever desire to engage in any sexual activity that I do not believe, feel or think is right.

57. My inner self does not believe that I should ever have any unwanted sexual desires related to anything that happened in the past.

58. My inner self is not interested in any sexual activity that it does not believe, feel or think is right.

59. My inner self does not believe that I should be interested in any sexual activity that I do not believe, feel or think is right.

60. My inner self has the willpower to resist engaging in any unwanted sexual activities.

61. My inner self does not have any unwanted sexual needs.

62. My inner self does not have any negative feelings, beliefs or thoughts directed towards anyone, for any reason.

63. My inner self believes that I should always protect myself from sexually transmitted diseases.

64. My inner self believes that I should always protect myself against unwanted pregnancies.

65. My inner self believes that I should always protect myself so that I do not impregnate someone that I do not want to impregnate.

66. My inner self does not have any negative thoughts or feelings about sex.

ELIMINATING SEXUAL DESIRES FOR CHILDREN

1. My inner self no longer desires to have sex with children and will never have that desire for any reason.

2. My inner self does not believe that I should ever desire to have sex with children.

3. My inner self does not, and will never, want to have sex with children, for any reason.

4. My inner self does not believe that I should ever want to have sex with children for any reason.

5. My inner self will never be sexually attracted to children for any reason.

6. My inner self does not believe that I should ever be sexually attracted to children.

7. My inner self will never have the urge to have sexual relations with children for any reason.

8. My inner self cannot be tempted to have sex with children for any reason.

9. My inner self never thinks about having sex with children for any reason.

10. My inner self does not believe that I should ever think about having sex with children.

11. My inner self will never harm children for any reason.

12. My inner self does not desire or want to sexually harm anyone for any reason.

13. My inner self does not want me to sexually assault anyone.

14. My inner self does not believe that I should sexually harm anyone.

15. My inner self does not want me to commit acts of violence.

16. My inner self has no desire, and will never desire, to view pornographic pictures or videos of children for any reason.

17. My inner self does not believe that I should ever desire to view pornographic pictures or videos of children for any reason.

18. My inner self does not believe that I should ever get any pleasure out of viewing pornographic pictures or videos of children for any reason.

19. My inner self will never desire to inappropriately make contact or touch children at any time, for any reason.

20. My inner self will never have any sexual interest in children for any reason.

21. My inner self does not believe that I should have any sexual interest in children.

22. All sexual desires for children have been permanently eliminated.

23. My inner self is always protective of children.

24. My inner self is never sexually attracted to children.

25. My inner self does not believe that I should ever be sexually attracted to children.

26. My inner self will never have uncontrollable urges to have sexual activities with children.

27. My inner self will never have any urges to have sexual activities with children.

28. My inner self believes that I should inform the authorities if I suspect or witness inappropriate sexual activities against children.

29. My inner self believes that I should seek help if I cannot control any sexual desire for children.

CHAPTER 5

Eliminating Addictions

ADDICTIONS

1. My inner self does not believe that I should have any unwanted habits or be addicted to anything.

2. My inner self believes that I am easily able to break any unwanted habit.

3. My inner self wants to break any unwanted habits and addictions.

4. My inner self believes that I can stop any unwanted habit or addiction at any time.

5. My inner self believes that I should feel that I have to stop any unwanted habit or addiction today.

6. My inner self does not believe that it should ever have a problem stopping any unwanted habit or addiction for any reason.

7. My inner self does not have a problem stopping any unwanted habit or addiction.

8. All desires, urges, and feelings to do things that I do not want to do have been eliminated.

9. My inner self does not believe that I should ever have urges to do things that I do not want to do.

10. My inner self believes that I will always have the strength to overcome easily any urge to do things that I do not want to do.

11. My inner self will always have the strength, willpower, motivation and determination to break any unwanted habit or addiction.

GAMBLING

1. My inner self does not believe that I should gamble excessively for any reason.

2. My inner self does not believe that I should gamble for any reason.

3. My inner self is not interested in gambling.

4. My inner self no longer desires to gamble.

5. All desires to gamble have been eliminated.

6. My inner self does not believe that I should ever have an urge to gamble.

7. My inner self does not believe that I should feel tempted to gamble.

8. My inner self has the willpower to stop gambling today and permanently.

9. I believe that I have the willpower to stop gambling today and permanently.

10. My inner self does not like to lose money or anything of value for any reason.

11. My inner self does not feel addicted to gambling.

12. My inner self does not believe that I should ever feel addicted to gambling.

13. My inner self does not believe that gambling is worth the risk.

14. My inner self does not believe in taking unnecessary chances.

15. My inner self does not believe that I should take any unnecessary chances.

16. My inner self does not want to gamble for any reason.

17. My inner self does not think that I should ever want to gamble.

18. My inner self believes that I should feel that I have to stop gambling today.

19. My inner self does not enjoy gambling.

20. My inner self does not believe that I should ever be affected in any way if I do not gamble.

21. My inner self will never miss gambling for any reason.

22. My inner self does not believe that I should ever miss gambling.

TOBACCO CESSATION (STOP SMOKING)

1. My inner self believes that I can stop smoking today and permanently.

2. My inner self does not believe that I should ever want to smoke for any reason.

3. My inner self does not believe that I should ever have the desire to smoke for any reason.

4. My inner self no longer has any desire to smoke.

5. All cravings and desires to smoke cigarettes, for any reason, have been permanently eliminated.

6. My inner self will never have any withdrawal symptoms when I stop smoking.

7. My inner self does not believe that I should ever have any withdrawal symptoms when I stop smoking.

8. My inner self will never get any pleasure from smoking.

9. My inner self has no interest in smoking.

10. My inner self does not believe that I should have any interest in smoking.

11. My inner self will always have the willpower to stop smoking.

12. My inner self will never smoke out of habit or routine.

13. My inner self believes, without a doubt, that I should stop smoking today and permanently.

14. My inner self will never crave cigarettes or nicotine for any reason.

15. My inner self does not believe that I should ever crave cigarettes or nicotine for any reason.

16. My inner self does not believe that I should ever enjoy the act of smoking.

17. My inner self will never be tempted to smoke for any reason.

18. My inner self believes that my addiction to cigarettes has been permanently eliminated.

19. My inner self does not doubt that it is possible to stop smoking today and never to smoke another cigarette again.

20. My inner self does not believe that I should doubt that it is possible to stop smoking today and permanently.

21. My inner self feels motivated and empowered to stop smoking today.

22. My inner self is in 100% agreement that I stop smoking cigarettes today and permanently.

23. My inner self never feels the need or desire to smoke for any reason.

24. My inner self does not have a smoking habit.

25. My inner self no longer enjoys, and never will enjoy, smoking cigarettes for any reason.

26. My inner self does not believe that I should ever enjoy smoking cigarettes.

27. My inner self will never have an urge to smoke cigarettes for any reason.

28. My inner self does not like the taste or smell of tobacco.

29. My inner self no longer desires or craves smoking cigarettes, and never will have that desire or craving, for any reason.

30. My inner self does not want me to smoke cigarettes for any reason.

31. My inner self believes that, without a doubt, I can stop smoking cigarettes today and permanently.

32. I believe that, without a doubt, I can stop smoking cigarettes today and permanently.

33. My inner self believes that I should feel that I have to stop smoking today.

34. My inner self feels emotionally and mentally balanced at all times.

35. My inner self does not believe that I need to smoke cigarettes for any reason.

36. My inner self does not believe that any pleasure I get from smoking one cigarette is worth the consequences.

37. My inner self does not believe that smoking one cigarette is worth the possible negative health consequences.

38. My inner self believes I have the willpower, determination and motivation to stop smoking today and permanently.

39. My inner self does not believe that I should miss smoking for any reason.

40. My inner self can always resist the temptation to smoke.

41. My inner self does not believe that I should feel tempted to smoke.

42. My inner self does not feel addicted to smoking.

43. My inner self no longer feels or believes that tobacco smoking is a habit.

44. My inner self never thinks about smoking.

45. My inner self does not believe that I should think about smoking.

46. My inner self can be around cigarettes and have no desire to smoke.

47. My inner self believes that I have no choice and that I must stop smoking today and permanently.

48. My inner self dislikes smoking.

49. My inner self cannot be influenced to smoke by anyone.

50. It is important to my inner self that I stop smoking today and permanently.

51. My inner self believes that it should be important to me to stop smoking today and permanently.

52. My inner self believes and feels that I have permanently broken the smoking habit.

ALCOHOL/ALCOHOLISM

1. My inner self does not have any desire to drink even a sip of alcohol.

2. My inner self does not believe that I should desire to drink even a sip of alcohol.

3. My inner self believes that I have no choice and that I must stop drinking alcohol today and permanently.

4. I believe, without a doubt, that I can stop drinking alcohol today and permanently.

5. My inner self is not apprehensive or afraid to stop drinking alcohol.

6. My inner self does not believe that I should be affected in any way when I stop drinking alcohol.

7. My inner self does not believe that I should have withdrawal symptoms.

8. My inner self dislikes drinking alcohol.

9. My inner self does not believe that I should enjoy the effect alcohol has on me.

10. It is important to my inner self that I stop drinking alcohol today and permanently.

11. My inner self believes that I should feel that I have to stop drinking alcohol today.

12. My inner self believes that it should be important to me to stop drinking alcohol today and permanently.

13. My inner self is no longer interested in drinking alcohol.

14. My inner self does not believe that I should ever drink alcohol to relieve stress.

15. My inner self does not believe that I should drink alcohol because everyone else is drinking.

16. My inner self cannot be influenced to drink alcohol for any reason.

17. My inner self will always be able to resist the temptation to drink alcohol.

18. My inner self does not believe that I am an alcoholic for life.

19. My inner self believes that I should feel good about not drinking alcohol.

20. My inner self believes that I can be around alcohol and not be tempted to drink.

21. My inner self believes that I can stop drinking alcohol today and permanently.

22. My inner self does not believe that I need to drink alcohol for any reason.

23. My inner self does not believe that I have to drink alcohol to be sociable.

24. My inner self believes that the overconsumption of alcohol is very dangerous to my health.

25. My inner self does not believe that I should ever drive a motor vehicle after drinking too much alcohol.

26. My inner self believes that I can always resist the urge, and the temptation, to drink alcohol.

27. My inner self does not believe that I should feel tempted to drink alcohol.

28. My inner self does not believe that I should drink any type of alcohol.

29. My inner self will never miss drinking alcohol for any reason.

30. My inner self does not think that I should ever miss drinking alcohol.

DRUG DEPENDENCY

1. All cravings for legal and illegal drugs have been permanently eliminated.

2. My inner self does not believe that I should crave or desire any legal or illegal drug for any reason.

3. My inner self does not crave or desire to use drugs for any reason.

4. My inner self does not believe that I should use drugs to feel good.

5. My inner self does not believe that I should use drugs to relieve stress.

6. My inner self does not believe that I should ever feel pressured to use drugs.

7. My inner self believes that I should feel that I have to stop using drugs today.

8. My inner self believes that I can break the addiction to any legal or illegal drug today and permanently.

9. My inner self does not believe that I should use legal or illegal drugs for recreational purposes for any reason.

10. My inner self believes that I have the willpower to stop using legal and illegal drugs today and permanently.

11. My inner self wants to stop using legal and illegal drugs.

12. My inner self believes that I should want to stop using drugs.

13. My inner self does not believe that I should ever be influenced to use drugs for any reason.

14. My inner self does not believe that I should feel tempted to use drugs.

15. My inner self does not believe that I should be afraid to stop using drugs.

16. My inner self does not believe that I should have any withdrawal symptoms related to ending any drug usage.

17. My inner self believes that I will always be able to resist any urge or temptation to use drugs.

18. My inner self believes that I can be around drugs without having the desire to use them.

19. My inner self has no desire to be around drugs or people who use drugs.

20. My inner self will never miss using drugs for any reason.

21. My inner self does not believe that I should ever miss using drugs.

CHAPTER 6

Success and Prosperity

PROSPERITY

1. My inner self believes that prosperity, success and wealth should only bring positive changes.

2. My inner self is always resourceful.

3. I believe that my inner self is resourceful.

4. My inner self believes that I will always be rewarded for my efforts.

5. My inner self will never be unproductive for any reason.

6. My inner self will always be productive.

7. My inner self believes that I should always be productive.

8. My inner self does not believe that there should ever be any obstacles preventing me from achieving my goals.

9. My inner self believes that I deserve to be prosperous and successful in everything.

10. My inner self will always be able to attract all the resources needed when they are needed.

11. My inner self believes that every aspect of my life will greatly improve.

12. My inner self always believes that I deserve to be happy, healthy, prosperous and strong.

13. My inner self believes that it is all right for me to have an abundance of everything.

14. My inner self desires to be prosperous.

15. My inner self believes that it can be prosperous in any undertaking.

16. My inner self believes that everyone deserves to be prosperous if he or she puts forth the effort.

17. My inner self believes that I should put forth the effort to be prosperous.

18. My inner self will never attempt to obtain prosperity, success or wealth in a dishonest manner for any reason.

19. My inner self believes that one should always share their prosperity.

20. My inner self believes that one should always be grateful for, and appreciative of, their prosperity.

21. My inner self does not believe that my success and prosperity should ever affect me in a negative way for any reason.

22. My inner self always believes that I should be successful and prosperous.

23. It is extremely important to my inner self that I become prosperous and successful.

24. It is important to my inner self that I make a lot of money.

25. It is extremely important to my inner self that I share my prosperity with those less fortunate.

26. It is extremely important to my inner self that I use my prosperity to help others.

27. It is extremely important to my inner self that I am never negatively changed when I become prosperous.

28. My inner self believes that there will always be opportunities that will enable me to become prosperous.

SUCCESS

1. My inner self believes that I will always be rewarded for my efforts.

2. My inner self will never be unproductive for any reason.

3. My inner self will always be productive.

4. My inner self does not believe that I should ever be unproductive.

5. My inner self believes that prosperity, success and wealth should only bring positive changes.

6. My inner self will never feel like a loser for any reason.

7. My inner self believes that I should always function at my best even under adverse conditions.

8. My inner self wants me to be successful.

9. My inner self believes that I deserve to be successful in everything.

10. My inner self does not believe that I should ever sabotage my own success.

11. My inner self is never indecisive for any reason.

12. My inner self does not believe that there should be any reasons why I should not be successful.

13. My inner self always has the drive and determination to be successful.

14. My inner self always has the drive and determination to accomplish anything.

15. My inner self believes that every aspect of my life will greatly improve.

16. My inner self always feels like doing the things that need to be done to be successful.

17. My inner self believes that I should always feel like doing the things that need to be done to be successful.

18. My inner self is all right with making sacrifices while on the road to success.

19. My inner self is always ambitious.

20. My inner self cares about me being successful and realizing all my dreams.

21. My inner self believes that it is very important to accomplish something positive and noteworthy.

22. My inner self does not believe in limitations.

23. My inner self believes that all things are possible.

24. My inner self does not believe that there are unsolvable problems.

25. My inner self believes that I can be successful in any undertaking.

26. My inner self does not always measure success by material things.

27. I am able to imagine myself being successful, happy and content.

28. I believe that my inner self has enough motivation to accomplish anything.

29. I believe that my inner self has enough intuition to accomplish anything.

30. I believe that my inner self has enough imagination to accomplish anything.

31. I believe that my inner self has enough discipline to accomplish anything.

32. I believe that my inner self has enough confidence to accomplish anything.

33. I believe that my inner self has enough drive to accomplish anything.

34. I believe that my inner self has enough energy to accomplish anything.

35. I believe that my inner self has enough faith to accomplish anything.

36. I believe that my inner self has enough creativity to accomplish anything.

37. I believe that my inner self has enough enthusiasm to accomplish anything.

38. I believe that my inner self has what it takes to accomplish anything.

39. I believe that my inner self has enough ambition to accomplish anything.

40. I believe that my inner self has enough skills and abilities to accomplish anything.

41. My inner self believes that prosperity, success and wealth should only bring positive changes.

LUCK

1. My inner self never feels unlucky or unfortunate for any reason.

2. My inner self does not believe that I should ever feel unlucky or unfortunate.

3. My inner self always feels lucky.

4. My inner self believes that I should always feel lucky.

Spirituality and Personal Outlook

METAPHYSICS

1. My inner self's spirit can never be broken for any reason.

2. My inner self's intuition can never be negatively affected by anyone or anything, for any reason.

3. My inner self is never negatively surprised by anything.

4. I believe that my inner self should always be altruistic.

5. My inner self is altruistic.

6. I believe that my inner self has been liberated from all karmic repercussions.

7. My inner self believes that I have been liberated from all karmic repercussions.

8. I believe that I have been liberated from all karmic repercussions.

9. I believe that my inner self has been forgiven of all sins.

10. My inner self believes that I have been forgiven of all sins.

11. I believe that I have been forgiven of all sins.

12. My inner self always feels blessed.

13. My inner self thinks that I should always feel blessed.

14. My inner self never lacks faith for any reason.

15. My inner self is always able to attract all that is good and repel all that is negative.

16. My inner self believes that my wishes and prayers will be fulfilled if it is in my best interests.

17. My inner self always feels that God is on its side.

18. I believe that God is on my side.

19. My inner self always guides me to do positive things and never negative things for any reason.

20. I believe my inner self is always working to find a solution to my problems.

21. My inner self is always working to find solutions to my problems.

22. My inner self does not believe that I should ever be self-sabotaging.

23. My inner self always feels mentally, emotionally and spiritually prepared for anything that may happen.

24. My inner self's spirit is never negatively affected by anyone or anything, for any reason.

25. My inner self never feels spiritually out of balance for any reason.

26. My inner self will never lose faith or hope for any reason.

27. My inner self does not believe that I should ever lose faith or hope for any reason.

28. My inner self has a good heart.

29. My inner self believes that I should always think positively.

30. My inner self believes that I should always feel positive.

31. My inner self's spirit is always positive.

32. My inner self's spirit is always happy.

WILLPOWER

1. My inner self has the willpower to accomplish anything.

2. I believe that I have the willpower to accomplish anything.

3. My inner self has the willpower to overcome anything.

4. I believe that I have the willpower to overcome anything.

5. I believe that I have the willpower to resist any temptation.

6. My inner self always has the willpower to resist any temptation.

7. There are no reasons why my inner self will not be able to resist any temptation.

8. My inner self does not believe that I should feel tempted to do anything that I should not do.

9. My inner self always has the willpower to resist anything that is not in its best interests.

10. My inner self believes that I should always have the willpower to resist anything that is not in my best interest.

EXPECTATIONS

1. My inner self is never negatively surprised by anything.

2. My inner self never expects bad or negative things to happen for any reason.

3. My inner self does not always feel as if something bad is about to happen.

4. My inner self does not believe that I should always expect negative things to happen.

5. My inner self does not believe that I should always feel that something bad will happen.

6. My inner self, although prepared for anything, always expects positive and good things to happen.

7. My inner self does not believe that I should ever try to live up to someone else's expectations for any reason.

8. My inner self never tries to live up to anyone's expectations for any reason.

9. My inner self always has positive expectations, never negative expectations.

10. My inner self is always expecting good things to happen.

GRATITUDE

1. My inner self believes that I should always express my gratitude.

2. My inner self believes that I should always be grateful and appreciative for all that I have.

3. My inner self believes that I should be grateful for everything that has been done for me.

4. My inner self believes that I should be grateful to everyone who has helped me in anyway.

5. My inner self believes that I should always show and express my gratitude and appreciation.

6. My inner self does not believe that I should ever take anyone or anything for granted.

IMAGINATION

1. My inner self is very imaginative.

2. My inner self can vividly imagine anything.

3. My inner self can use its imagination to solve all my problems.

4. My inner self can use its imagination to enhance every aspect of my life.

5. My inner self can use its imagination to come up with unique and creative ideas.

6. My inner self is able to imagine anything.

7. My imagination will never negatively affect me.

8. My inner self's imagination can never be negatively influenced for any reason.

9. My inner self always has complete control over its imagination.

10. My inner self believes that I should always have complete control over my imagination.

11. My inner self never imagines anything negative.

12. My inner self believes that I should always imagine positive things.

13. My inner self can vividly imagine all things.

ATTRACTION

1. My inner self will always be able to attract all the resources that I need, when I need them.

2. My inner self will always attract everything that I need and want, as long as it is in my best interest.

3. My inner self never attracts anything negative for any reason.

4. My inner self is never attracted to negative people or things for any reason.

5. My inner self always attracts positive things and repels negative things.

LIMITATIONS

1. My inner self never believes in limitations.

2. My inner self does not believe that I should ever believe in limitations

3. My inner self's thoughts are never limiting.

4. My inner self does not believe that any of my thoughts should ever be limiting.

HEALING

1. My inner self is able to recover rapidly from any illness.

2. I believe that my body can heal itself of all disorders.

3. My inner self believes that I am able to recover fully from any disorder.

4. My inner self does not believe that there should be any reasons why I should not recover completely from any disorder.

5. My inner self does not doubt that I will recover completely.

6. My inner self thinks that I should always believe that I will be completely healed, physically, mentally, emotionally and spiritually, of all disorders.

7. My inner self believes that I should always take it upon myself to remain healthy.

8. My inner self believes that I should do what is necessary to get well and stay well.

ATTITUDES

1. My inner self's attitude will always be positive and never negative for any reason.

2. My inner self believes that I should always have a positive attitude.

3. My inner self always has a positive attitude and positive disposition.

4. My inner self's attitude is never negatively affected by anyone or anything for any reason.

DEATH

1. My inner self never thinks about death or dying for any reason.

2. My inner self does not believe that I should think about death or dying.

3. My inner self does not believe that I should think about death or dying after awakening from sleep.

4. My inner self will never fear death for any reason.

5. My inner self does not believe that I should be afraid of dying.

6. My inner self is not afraid of dying.

7. My inner self is not afraid of the afterlife.

8. My inner self is not afraid of what will become of my loved ones once I make my transition.

9. My inner self does not believe that I should worry about what will become of my loved ones once I make my transition.

10. My inner self believes that I should feel confident that everyone will be all right and will manage without me.

11. My inner self does not have any negative thoughts about dying and what will become of me after I die.

12. My inner self does not look upon death as the end of my existence.

13. I do not look upon death as the end of my existence.

14. My inner self does not believe that I should ever wish to die before my time.

15. My inner self does not believe that I should wish that anyone would have an untimely death.

16. My inner self believes that I should be able to talk about death without the discussion having a negative effect on me.

17. My inner self does not wish for anyone to grieve when I make my transition, for any reason.

18. My inner self believes that I should feel certain that there is life after death.

19. My inner self believes that I should feel certain that I will have a better life after death.

20. My inner self believes that my loved ones will have a better life after death.

21. My inner self believes that I will be eventually reunited with all my friends, family and loved ones after death.

DREAMS

1. My inner self is never negatively affected by dreams for any reason.

2. My inner self does not believe that I should ever be negatively affected by dreams.

3. My inner self believes that my dreams should either have a positive effect on me or none at all.

4. My inner self believes that all of my dream characters should be positive and on my side.

5. My inner self does not believe that any harm should come to me in my dreams.

6. My inner self's dreams are always positive, never negative.

7. My inner self believes that all my dreams should be positive.

8. My inner self does not believe that I should have nightmares.

9. My inner self does not believe that I should be afraid while dreaming or when I awaken from a dream.

10. My inner self does not believe that I should have recurrent negative dreams.

11. My inner self does not believe that I should dream of past traumatic events.

12. My inner self does not believe that my dreams should negatively change the way that I feel.

13. I will never be afraid to go to sleep because of my dreams.

14. No one in my dreams will ever be able to influence negatively my inner self or me at any time.

15. I believe that my dreams should be fun, exciting and informative.

MATTERS OF THE HEART

1. My inner self's heart is completely free of pain and suffering.

2. My inner self believes that my heart should be completely free of all pain and suffering.

3. My inner self's heart never feels broken for any reason.

4. My heart no longer feels broken.

5. My heart is not broken.

6. My inner self's heart is not broken.

7. My inner self's heart is pure.

8. My inner self's heart is free of all negative emotions.

9. All traces of hate have been removed from my heart.

10. My inner self has a good and unselfish heart.

HOPE

1. My inner self will never lose hope for any reason.

2. My inner self does not believe that I should ever lose hope for any reason.

FAITH

1. My inner self will never lose faith for any reason.

2. My inner self does not believe that I should ever lose faith for any reason.

TRUST

1. My inner self never distrusts everyone.

2. My inner self is able to trust.

3. My inner self believes that I should always be trustworthy.

4. My inner self does not believe that I should ever lose trust in everyone.

5. My inner self believes that I should trust, but always be aware that not everyone can be trusted.

6. I believe that my inner self knows who can be trusted and who cannot be trusted.

7. My inner self will always guide me as to whom I can trust and whom I cannot trust.

OBSTACLES

1. I believe that my inner self can overcome all obstacles.

2. My inner self believes that I can overcome all obstacles.

3. There will never be an obstacle that my inner self cannot overcome for any reason.

4. My inner self does not believe that I should allow any obstacle to prevent me from achieving my goals, unless my goals were not meant to be.

Negative Behavior

INTIMIDATION AND BULLYING

1. My inner self does not believe that I should ever be intimidated by anyone, for any reason.

2. My inner self is never intimidated for any reason.

3. My inner self never feels intimidated for any reason.

4. My inner self does not believe that I should intimidate anyone for any reason.

5. My inner self never feels ridiculed for any reason.

6. My inner self does not believe that other people's thoughts, feelings, emotions, words or actions should affect me in a negative way for any reason.

7. My inner self cannot be bullied.

8. My inner self does not believe that I should allow myself to be bullied.

9. My inner self does not believe that I should bully anyone, for any reason.

10. My inner self does not believe that I should ever care about what people say or think about me for any reason.

11. My inner self is never afraid to stand up to anyone.

12. My inner self is never fearful.

13. My inner self is never afraid to talk to anyone about me being bullied.

14. My inner self does not believe that I should feel ashamed or embarrassed about being bullied.

15. My inner self never feels powerless or helpless.

16. My inner self does not think that I should ever feel powerless or helpless for any reason.

ANTI-SOCIAL BEHAVIOR

1. My inner self is not violent or destructive, and will never be violent or destructive for any reason.

2. My inner self does not believe that I should ever be violent or destructive.

3. My inner self does not believe that I should feel or be combative.

4. My inner self does not believe that I should feel or think negatively for any reason.

5. My inner self does not want to harm, hurt or assault anyone for any reason.

6. My inner self only fights in self-defense or in defense of someone else.

7. My inner self does not want to kill anyone for any reason.

8. My inner self is not, and will never be, angry, mean or evil for any reason.

9. My inner self is kind and considerate.

10. My inner self is not, and will not be, revengeful or vindictive for any reason.

11. My inner self is not, and will never be, hostile or bitter for any reason.

12. My inner self values its own life and the lives of others.

13. My inner self is not selfish.

14. My inner self will always be caring and compassionate.

15. My inner self prefers to be honest.

16. My inner self is honest.

17. My inner self prefers to settle disputes nonviolently.

18. My inner self is not angry with anyone.

19. My inner self is never negative for any reason.

20. My inner self never hates anyone for any reason.

21. All traces of hate have been removed from my inner self.

22. My inner self loves me.

23. My inner self loves itself.

24. My inner self does not believe in stealing or robbing for any reason.

25. My inner self respects other people's property.

26. My inner self will never be cold, heartless or insensitive for any reason.

27. My inner self will never feel cold, heartless or insensitive for any reason.

28. My inner self is not, and will never be, negatively aggressive for any reason.

29. My inner self never loses control of its emotions or temper for any reason.

30. My inner self does not enjoy violence and is not attracted to anything negative.

31. My inner self never feels, and will never feel, like an animal, beast or monster for any reason.

32. My inner self never enjoys, and will never enjoy, seeing others suffer for any reason.

33. My inner self is not, and will not be, interested in anything evil or violent for any reason.

34. My inner self is always respectful of others.

35. My inner self does not want me to commit acts of violence.

36. My inner self cannot be influenced to commit acts of violence.

37. My inner self does not believe that I should be negatively influenced by anything or anyone.

38. My inner self does not believe that I should be negatively influenced by violent or negative movies or television shows.

39. My inner self does not believe that I should be negatively influenced by violent or negative games.

40. My inner self does not believe that I should be negatively influenced by violent or negative music.

41. My inner self does not believe that violent or negative things that I experienced in the past should negatively influence me.

42. My inner self does not want me to harm anyone in any way, except in the case of self-defense.

43. My inner self does not want me to take that which is not mine.

44. My inner self does not believe that I should be influenced to do anything that I feel is not right.

45. My inner self believes that I should always take personal responsibility for my actions.

CHAPTER 9

Eliminating Counter-productive Personality Traits

INABILITY TO ADAPT

1. I believe that my inner self is adaptable.

2. My inner self believes that I should always be adaptable.

3. There are no reasons why my inner self is unable to adapt to any situation.

4. My inner self totally agrees with all positive changes that have been made.

5. My inner self is always adaptable.

6. I am adaptable.

INABILITY TO DEAL WITH CHANGE

1. My inner self is never against changing for the better for any reason.

2. My inner self never resists any necessary changes for any reason.

3. My inner self does not believe that I should ever be resistant to positive changes.

4. My inner self does not believe that I should be resistant to change.

5. My inner self is always open to changing and improving the way that things are done.

6. My inner self does not believe that I should follow the same routine everyday and be opposed to changing.

7. My inner self is never resistant to positive changes for any reason.

8. My inner self is always open to positive changes.

9. My inner self is never negatively affected if things are done outside of a regular routine.

10. My inner self is always changing for the better.

CONTROL ISSUES

1. My inner self cannot be negatively controlled or influenced by anyone at any time, for any reason.

2. My inner self does not want to be controlled.

3. My inner self can never be controlled by sex at any time, for any reason.

4. My inner self will never be controlled by any desires for any reason.

5. My inner self can never be negatively influenced by anything or anyone, for any reason.

6. My inner self does not believe that I should ever have impulses that I cannot control.

7. My inner self never has uncontrollable impulses.

8. My inner self does not believe that I should allow anyone to control me emotionally.

9. My inner self never has the desire to control anyone.

10. My inner self does not feel that it always has to be completely in control over someone.

11. My inner self does not believe that I have to be the one who has to be completely in control of everything.

12. My inner self does not mind relinquishing control when appropriate.

13. My inner self does not believe that I should mind relinquishing control when appropriate.

14. My inner self will not allow itself to be controlled or manipulated by anyone or anything.

RELUCTANCE

1. My inner self is never reluctant to do anything that needs to be done for any reason.

2. My inner self does not believe that I should ever be reluctant to do anything that needs to be done.

CHAPTER 10

Governing
Your State of Mind

CONTROLLING
YOUR INTERESTS AND DESIRES

1. My inner self will never lose interest in all things for any reason.

2. My inner self does not believe that I should lose interest in all things.

3. My inner self believes that I should be interested in all things that will further my growth and development.

4. My inner self does not believe that I should be interested in anything that is negative or counterproductive.

5. My inner self believes that I should always be interested in doing new things.

6. My inner self believes that I should always be interested in learning new things.

7. My inner self believes that I should always be interested in learning new skills.

8. My inner self does not believe that I should ever lose interest in anything because of my age.

PROPER MOODS

1. My inner self is never in a mood where it does not want to do anything.

2. My inner self does not believe that I should ever be in a mood where I do not want to do anything.

3. My inner self is never in a negative mood for any reason.

4. My inner self's mood is never negatively affected for any reason.

5. My inner self is always in the mood to do what needs to be done.

6. My inner self is always in a positive mood.

7. My inner self believes that I should always be in a positive mood.

8. My inner self is not moody.

9. My inner self's mood is always stable.

10. My inner self's mood cannot be negatively affected by anyone or anything.

CHAPTER 11

Insomnia

OVERCOMING INSOMNIA

1. My inner self does not believe that I should be thinking about anything when going to sleep.

2. My inner self's mind is always calm and relaxed.

3. My inner self believes that I should be able to sleep soundly under any condition.

4. My inner self does not believe that worrying will accomplish anything.

5. My inner self does not think that I should worry about anything while falling asleep.

6. My inner self's mind is free of all worries.

7. My inner self believes that my mind should always be free of all worries.

8. My inner self believes that I should be able to sleep without constantly waking up.

9. My inner self believes that if I awaken I should easily be able to go back to sleep.

10. My inner self does not believe that my dreams should be negative or frightening.

11. My inner self believes that I should sleep six, seven or eight hours nightly.

12. My inner self does not believe that I should be thinking about anything, for any reasons, when attempting to go to sleep.

13. My inner self believes that I should always look forward to going to sleep.

14. My inner self thinks that I should awaken only in the case of an emergency.

15. My inner self will awaken me in the case of an emergency.

16. My inner self does not believe that I should worry or be afraid of anything while I am sleeping.

17. My inner self does not think that I should have a difficult time falling asleep.

18. My inner self thinks that I should relax and go to sleep.

Children and Young Adults: Growing Into a Happy, Healthy and Fully Functional Adult

GENERAL

1. My inner self believes that being happy and successful should be numbers one and two on my priority list.

2. My inner self believes that I should be kind and considerate, especially with family members.

3. My inner self believes that I should be polite and respectful, especially with family members.

4. My inner self is always adaptable.

5. My inner self believes that I should always be adaptable.

6. My inner self believes that I should always be patient and understanding.

7. My inner self believes that I should always be tolerant.

8. My inner self does not envy anyone for any reason.

9. My inner self always has a positive attitude about all things.

10. My inner self never feels abandoned.

11. My inner self never feels intimidated.

12. My inner self will never be passive.

13. My inner self does not believe in being taken advantage of and does not think that I should ever allow someone to take advantage of me.

14. My inner self never feels threatened by anyone.

15. My inner self is not overly defensive or argumentative.

16. My inner self does not believe that I should be negatively affected if anyone talks to me in a way that I do not like.

17. My inner self does not believe that I should feel or think negatively for any reason.

18. My inner self does not think that today is going to be a stressful day.

STATE OF MIND

1. My inner self always has a positive attitude and disposition and is never negative for any reason.

2. My inner self believes that I should always have a positive attitude and disposition.

3. My inner self never feels stressed for any reason.

4. My inner self does not believe that I should ever feel stressed for any reason.

5. My inner self never feels depressed for any reason.

6. My inner self never feels sad for any reason.

7. My inner self does not believe that I should ever feel sad or depressed for any reason.

8. My inner self does not fear the future.

9. My inner self values my life and values being healthy.

10. My inner self believes that I should always value my life and value being healthy.

11. My inner self never worries about anything for any reason.

12. My inner self does not believe that I should ever worry about anything for any reason.

13. My inner self does not believe that I should ever feel overwhelmed by schoolwork.

14. My inner self is not angry, hostile or bitter about anything.

15. My inner self never feels angry, rebellious or hostile for any reason.

16. My inner self does not believe that I should ever feel angry, rebellious or hostile.

17. My inner self does not believe that I should lose my temper, for any reason, especially with my family members.

18. My inner self feels safe and secure.

19. My inner self is not afraid of the dark.

20. My inner self is not afraid of being alone.

21. My inner self is not afraid of dying.

22. My inner self never thinks about dying.

23. My inner self always feels loved.

24. My inner self believes that I will be successful and prosperous if I put forth the effort.

25. My inner self never feels disappointed for any reason.

26. My inner self does not feel like crying.

27. My inner self will never feel abandoned or unloved for any reason.

28. My inner self always feels emotionally and mentally balanced.

29. My inner self never feels bored.

30. My inner self believes that I should feel neutral to all bad memories and experiences.

31. My inner self feels neutral to all bad memories and experience.

32. My inner self does not believe that I should be negatively affected by anything that happened in the past.

33. My inner self will always have the will to survive.

34. My inner self does not believe that I should be negatively affected if anyone disagrees with me.

35. My inner self believes that I should always feel happy and in control.

36. My inner self believes that I should always think positively.

37. My inner self believes that I should always feel positive.

38. My inner self's spirit is always positive.

39. My inner self's spirit is always happy.

PARENTS

1. My inner self always believes that I should be respectful towards others, especially my parents.

2. My inner self believes that I should value others' advice and guidance, especially my parents and caretakers.

3. My inner self believes that I should be respectful of my parents' age, knowledge and experience.

4. My inner self does not believe that I should be negatively affected if my parents disagree with me.

5. My inner self does not believe that I should desire to do the opposite of what my parents desire.

6. My inner self believes that I should be open to compromise when necessary.

7. My inner self does not believe that I should be negatively affected if my parents talk to me in a way that I do not like.

8. My inner self believes that it is important that I let my parents and caretakers know how much I care about them, love them, and appreciate all that they have done for me.

LOVE, TRUST AND GRATITUDE

1. My inner self is always thankful and appreciative.

2. My inner self believes that I should forgive everyone who has harmed me in the past.

3. My inner self has forgiven everyone of everything. I have forgiven everyone of everything.

4. My inner self believes that I have been forgiven of everything.

5. My inner self is never distrusting of everyone.

6. My inner self believes that I should be trusting, but aware that not everyone can be trusted.

7. My inner self is trusting but cautious.

8. My inner self is always grateful and appreciative.

9. My inner self does not believe that I should ever take anyone or anything for granted.

SELF-ESTEEM

1. My inner self believes that I should always feel good about myself.

2. My inner self believes that I should always love others and myself.

3. My inner self feels confident and competent.

4. My inner self feels good about itself and believes that I should feel good about myself.

5. My inner self believes that it is all right for me to be myself always.

6. My inner self does not feel that anyone is talking about me or making fun of me and, truthfully, it does not care even if they are doing so.

7. My inner self believes that I should always feel good about myself.

8. My inner self is not shy and does not believe I should feel shy.

9. My inner self loves me. I love myself.

10. My inner self will never feel hopeless or powerless.

11. My inner self always feels smart.

12. My inner self feels attractive. I feel attractive.

13. My inner self does not believe that I should ever feel or think that I am unattractive for any reason.

14. My inner self is proud of everything about me.

15. My inner self believes that I should always be proud of myself.

16. My inner self never feels ashamed or embarrassed about anything.

17. My inner self does not believe that I should feel ashamed or embarrassed about anything.

18. My inner self believes that I should feel comfortable with me being me.

19. My inner self does not believe that I should seek acceptance or approval from anyone to feel good about myself.

20. My inner self does not think that anyone is better than I am.

21. My inner self will never have a problem with being rejected for any reason.

22. My inner self does not feel the need to please everyone all the time.

23. My inner self believes that I should always feel proud of my race and my ancestors.

CONFIDENCE

1. My inner self is never afraid of failure.

2. My inner self is not afraid of making mistakes.

3. My inner self is not afraid of messing up.

4. My inner self always feels that I am capable of doing anything.

5. My inner self always feels confident.

RESISTANCE TO OUTSIDE INFLUENCES

1. My inner self is never negatively influenced by anyone, for any reason.

2. My inner self does not believe that I should be negatively influenced by anyone or anything, for any reason.

3. My inner self does not believe that I should be negatively influenced by violent or negative movies or television shows.

4. My inner self does not believe that I should be negatively influenced by violent or negative games.

5. My inner self does not believe that I should be negatively influenced by violent or negative music.

6. My inner self does not believe that violent or negative things that I experienced in the past should negatively influence me.

7. My inner self does not believe that I should ever feel pressured to do anything that I do not feel is right.

8. My inner self does not believe that I should ever feel pressured to do anything that I do not think is right.

9. My inner self never feels pressured.

10. My inner self does not believe that I should ever feel pressured.

11. My inner self is never negatively affected by what other people think or say about me.

12. My inner self does not believe that I should ever be negatively affected by what other people think or say about me.

13. My inner self never feels pressured to drink alcohol.

14. My inner self does not believe that I should ever feel pressured to drink alcohol.

15. My inner self never feels pressured to use drugs.

16. My inner self does not believe that I should ever feel pressured to use drugs.

17. My inner self never feels pressured to smoke cigarettes.

18. My inner self does not believe that I should ever feel pressured to smoke cigarettes.

19. My inner self never feels pressured to engage in sexual activities.

20. My inner self does not believe that I should ever feel pressured to engage in sexual activities.

21. My inner self is never negatively affected by anyone or anything, for any reason.

22. My inner self does not believe that I should ever have a problem saying "no" to something that I do not want to do or should not do.

23. My inner self does not believe that I should feel tempted to do anything that I should not do.

24. My inner self cannot be negatively influenced to do anything that it feels is not right.

SELF CONTROL

1. My inner self believes that I should always have complete control of all my desires, including sexual desires.

2. My inner self does not believe that I should engage in any sexual activities at this time of my life.

3. My inner self believes that I should be more focused on my self-development than on sex or my sexual orientation.

4. My inner self is not easily distracted.

5. My inner self does not believe that I should be easily distracted.

6. My inner self will never desire to harm anyone, including me, for any reason.

7. My inner self does not believe that I should be angry, irritated or annoyed by any of my family members.

8. My inner self does not believe that I should allow myself to become angry, irritated or annoyed for any reason.

9. My inner self believes that I should always feel happy and in control.

DESIRE TO SUCCEED

1. My inner self always feels special.

2. My inner self is always focused and determined to do the things that need to be done.

3. My inner self always feels motivated to do the things that need to be done.

4. My inner self always believes that I should strive to be successful.

5. My inner self does not think that anyone is better than I am.

6. My inner self will never have a problem with being rejected for any reason.

7. My inner self does not believe that rejection or the fear of rejection should ever discourage or deter me from accomplishing my goals.

8. My inner self is motivated to excel at all things.

9. My inner self believes that I should always feel like doing the things that need to be done.

10. My inner self does not think that any aspect of school is stressful.

11. My inner self does not believe that I should feel stressed when taking tests.

12. My inner self believes that I should always feel like doing my homework.

13. My inner self believes that I should always be excited and enthusiastic about learning new things.

INTEGRITY

1. My inner self always feels remorseful when I do something that is not right.

2. My inner self believes that I should always feel remorseful when I do something that I know is not right.

3. My inner self believes that I should always be apologetic and forgiving.

4. My inner self does not believe that I have to use profanity to express myself.

5. My inner self is not prejudiced or discriminatory and does not believe that I should ever be prejudiced or discriminatory for any reason.

Successful Parenting

BEING A LOVING, WISE AND EFFECTIVE PARENT

1. My inner self is always patient and understanding.

2. My inner self believes that I should always be patient and understanding.

3. My inner self believes that I should always be patient and understanding with my child.

4. My inner self believes that I should be open to compromise when necessary.

5. My inner self does not believe that I should feel frustrated with my child for any reason.

6. My inner self does not believe that I should be negatively affected if my child talks to me in a way that I do not like.

7. My inner self does not believe that I should be angry with my child.

8. My inner self does not believe that I should lose my temper with my child for any reason.

9. My inner self does not believe that I should ever be disappointed with my child for any reason.

10. My inner self does not believe that I should ever have unrealistic expectations of my child.

11. My inner self does not believe that I should ever push my child too hard.

12. My inner self believes that I should always be respectful and honest with my child.

13. My inner self does not believe that I should ever be overly critical for any reason.

14. My inner self does not believe that I should unfairly favor one child over another one of my children.

15. My inner self does not believe that I should ever be negatively affected by my child.

16. My inner self does not believe that worrying ever accomplishes anything.

17. My inner self does not believe that I should worry about my child's safety.

18. My inner self does not believe that I should worry about my child's future.

19. My inner self does not believe that I should worry about my child's grades.

20. My inner self does not believe that I should worry about what school my child will attend.

21. My inner self does not believe that I should worry about my child's health.

22. My inner self does not worry about anyone, for any reason.

23. My inner self does not believe that I should worry about anyone or anything, for any reason.

24. My inner self believes that I should think, feel and believe that my child will be all right.

25. My inner self always expects positive things to happen, but is mentally, emotionally, physically and spiritually prepared for anything that could possibly happen to my child.

26. My inner self believes that I am prepared, mentally, emotionally, physically and spiritually, for anything that could possibly happen to my child.

27. My inner self believes that I should always do as much as I possibly can to ensure that my child will be all right.

28. My inner self believes that I should always allow my child a healthy amount of independence.

29. My inner self believes that I should always be loving and supportive.

30. My inner self believes that I should always be available for my child.

31. My inner self does not believe that I should ever be too strict or too lenient with my child.

32. My inner self does not believe that I should allow my child to make me feel angry, irritated or annoyed, for any reason.

33. My inner self thinks that my child should be 100% certain that I always care.

34. My inner self believes that my child should always know that we are on the same team.

35. My inner self believes that I should always make my child feel loved.

36. My inner self is never stressed for any reason.

37. My inner self does not believe that I should ever be stressed for any reason.

38. My inner self does not believe that I should let my child make me feel stressed or overwhelmed for any reason.

39. My inner self does not believe that I should ever have any negative thoughts or feelings related to my child for any reason.

40. My inner self does not believe that I should ever be jealous of my child for any reason.

41. My inner self does not believe that I should ever have a competitive relationship with my child.

42. My inner self believes that I should always be protective of my child, but never overly protective.

43. My inner self believes that I should always behave around my child in the way that I would like for them to behave.

44. My inner self does not believe that I should burden my child with my problems.

45. My inner self does not believe that I should harm my child in anyway.

46. My inner self does not believe that I should intimidate my child.

47. My inner self does not believe that I should be intimidated by my child.

48. My inner self does not believe that I should make my child fear me.

49. My inner self does not believe that I should fear my child.

50. My inner self does not believe that I should have a problem saying "no" to my child when appropriate.

51. My inner self does not believe that I should be negatively affected if my child disagrees with me.

52. My inner self is not negatively affected if anyone disagrees with me.

53. My inner self is never affected, for any reason, if someone disagrees with me.

54. My inner self does not believe that raising children is stressful.

55. My inner self does not believe that I should feel that raising children is stressful.

56. My inner self believes that I should always do the best that I can with raising my child and never blame myself if my child does not live up to my expectations.

57. My inner self does not believe that I should be sad or depressed when it is time for my child to leave home.

58. My inner self believes that I should always give generously of my time.

59. My inner self believes that I should always enjoy taking care of my child, even when they are adults.

60. My inner self believes that I should always enjoy being a parent.

61. My inner self believes that it is a blessing to be a parent.

Relationships

MAINTAINING A LOVING, HAPPY AND SUCCESSFUL RELATIONSHIP

1. My inner self believes that I should always go into any relationship with good intentions.

2. My inner self is completely over all previous relationships, has forgiven everyone, and has moved on.

3. My inner self believes that I should be completely over all previous relationships before starting a new one.

4. My inner self believes that I should always be respectful and considerate of my companion.

5. My inner self believes that I should always be respectful of my companion's opinions, desires and needs.

6. My inner self believes that I should always be thoughtful.

7. My inner self believes that I should always be fair and just.

8. My inner self believes that I should be completely trusting when I feel my companion is trustworthy.

9. My inner self believes that I should be trustworthy.

10. My inner self believes that I should always be honest with my companion.

11. My inners self believes that I should always be sensitive of my companion's feelings.

12. My inners self does not believe that I should ever be overly sensitive for any reason.

13. My inner self believes that I should always be patient and understanding.

14. My inner self believes that I should always be tolerant and flexible.

15. My inner self believes that I should always be generous with my time.

16. My inner self believes that I should always be concerned and caring.

17. My inner self believes that I should always be supportive during both good times and bad times.

18. My inner self believes that, if agreed upon, I should only have one companion and always be faithful.

19. My inner self believes that I should always be forgiving.

20. My inner self believes that I should be open to compromise when necessary.

21. My inner self believes that the lines of communication should always be open.

22. My inner self does not believe that I should ever have a problem expressing my opinion or emotions.

23. My inner self believes that my companion should always be well aware of how much I care about her/him.

24. Repeat the following affirmation if the relationship has evolved to the level of Love, if not move on to the next affirmation: My inner self believes that my companion should always know and feel that I love her/him.

25. My inner self believes that, if the feeling is mutual, we should strive to grow and develop together, and stay together for always.

26. My inner self does not believe that the relationship should ever be competitive in nature for any reason.

27. My inner self does not believe that I should ever be envious or jealous of my companion for any reason.

28. My inner self does not believe that I should be selfish or self-centered.

29. My inner self does not believe that I should ever feel intimidated by my companion for any reason.

30. My inner self does not believe that I should ever intimidate my companion for any reason.

31. My inner self does not believe that I should ever work against my companion.

32. My inner self does not believe that I should ever be negatively influenced by others outside of the relationship.

33. My inner self does not believe that I should be dishonest or deceitful for any reason.

34. My inner self does not believe that I should ever be too demanding or critical for any reason.

35. My inner self does not believe that I should ever treat my companion negatively in any way, for any reason.

36. My inner self does not believe that I should ever neglect my companion.

37. My inner self does not believe that I should bring any negative feelings, thoughts or beliefs from previous relationships into the present relationship.

38. My inner self does not believe that I should blame my present companion for anything that happened in previous relationships.

39. My inner self does not believe that I should ever take advantage of my companion for any reason.

40. My inner self does not believe that I should allow myself to be taken advantage of by anyone.

41. My inner self does not believe that I should harm my companion in any way, for any reason.

42. My inner self does not believe that I should ever abuse my companion in any way, for any reason.

43. My inner self does not believe that I should stay in an abusive relationship for any reason.

44. My inner self does not believe that I should ever lose my temper with my companion for any reason.

45. My inner self does not believe that I should ever stay angry with my companion for any reason.

46. My inner self does not believe that I should ever humiliate or belittle my companion.

47. My inner self is never negatively affected by disagreements.

48. My inner self does not believe that I should ever have a problem agreeing or disagreeing with my companion.

49. My inner self does not believe that I should be negatively affected if my companion disagrees with me.

50. My inner self would like good relationships to last forever, but it is aware that sometimes a relationship must end due to various circumstances.

51. My inner self will not be negatively affected if the relationship ends.

52. My inner self does not believe that I should be negatively affected if the relationship ends.

53. My inner self does not believe that I should ever become sad or depressed if the relationship ever ends.

54. My inner self does not believe that I should ever hold any ill feelings for my former companion.

55. My inner self does not believe that I should ever hate my companion or former companion.

56. My inner self does not believe that I should ever attempt to harm my former companion in any way.

57. My inner self does not believe that I should ever be unfair, vindictive or revengeful, for any reason, if the relationship ends.

58. My inner self does not believe that I should be angry with anyone or blame anyone if the relationship ends.

59. My inner self does not believe that I should turn our child against my companion.

60. My inner self does not believe that I should ever use our child against my companion.

61. My inner self does not believe that I should hold onto any ill feelings after the breakup.

62. My inner self believes that I should let go and move on after the relationship ends.

63. My inner self does not believe that any relationship should negatively influence future relationships.

64. My inner self no longer has any negative thoughts related to my companion or former companion.

65. My inner self does not believe that I should ever be affected by whomever my companion dates after our relationship is over.

66. My inner self does not feel any emotional pain or suffering related to the relationship.

67. All emotional pain and suffering related to the past relationship has been eliminated.

68. My inner self does not believe that I should ever suffer, for any reason, in connection to any relationship.

69. My inner self believes that if irreconcilable offenses were not committed, and if the feeling is mutual, I should always be open to reconcile.

70. My inner self believes that I deserve to be in a loving, happy and successful relationship.

71. My inner self believes that my perfect companion and I will find each other.

CHAPTER 15

Aging Concerns

FEELING YOUNG FOREVER

1. My inner self does not believe that I should ever feel unmotivated for any reason.

2. My inner self will never fear aging.

3. My inner self never feels too old to do anything.

4. I do not believe that my inner self should feel too old to do anything, for any reason.

5. My inner self always believes it is capable of doing all of the things that it did while younger.

6. My inner self believes that I should be able to enjoy doing the same things that I did while I was younger.

7. My inner self will never feel old for any reason.

8. My inner self does not believe that I should ever feel old for any reason.

9. My inner self does not believe that I should slow down because I am getting older.

10. My inner self does not believe that I should become weak as I get older.

11. My inner self does not believe that I should become forgetful.

12. My inner self does not believe that I should limit myself, in any way, because of my age.

13. My inner self believes that I should always feel young and full of energy.

14. My inner self does not believe that I should feel old for any reason.

15. My inner self does not believe that I should have any negative thoughts about aging.

16. My inner self believes that I should always feel good about my age and myself.

17. My inner self does not believe that I should use my age as an excuse for not doing anything.

18. My inner self does not believe that I should ever worry about dying or about how much time I have left before I make my transition.

19. My inner self does not believe that my life is passing by too fast.

20. My inner self believes that I should continue to grow and develop.

21. My inner self believes that I should remain active.

22. My inner self believes that I should continue to learn and to acquire new skills.

23. My inner self believes that I will always be valuable and that I have a lot to contribute.

24. My inner self believes that I should see every day as a new beginning.

25. My inner self believes that I can be healthy, vibrant and energetic at any age.

26. My inner self believes that I should feel good about myself.

27. My inner self believes that I look appealing, and I believe that I look appealing.

28. My inner self believes that I look appealing to others.

29. My inner self believes that my age and experience puts me at an advantage.

30. My inner self believes that I should always feel and act young.

31. My inner self believes that I am physically attractive.

32. My inner self never thinks that it is getting old and cannot do the things that it did in the past for any reason.

33. My inner self does not believe that I should think that I am getting old and cannot do the things that I did in the past.

34. My inner self does not believe that I should let anything that happened, or that did not happen, in the past negatively influence me in any way.

35. My inner self will always think and feel young.

36. My inner self always feels youthful.

37. My inner self feels playful.

38. My inner self believes that I can stay young forever.

39. My inner self will always be young.

Pain Management

GENERAL PAIN AND HEADACHES

1. My inner self believes that all pain can be permanently and instantly eliminated.

2. My inner self believes that my pain will decrease in intensity and go away completely.

3. My inner self does not believe that I should have pain in any part of body for any reason.

4. My inner self believes that I should always have a high pain threshold.

5. My inner self believes that I should have a high tolerance for pain.

6. My inner self believes that all soreness, stiffness and inflammation will decrease in intensity and go away completely.

7. My inner self does not believe that I should have headaches for any reason.

8. My inner self believes that pain and pressure in my head will go away completely.

9. My inner self believes that the tension in my head will go away completely.

10. My inner self does not believe that I should periodically get headaches for any reason.

11. My inner self does not believe that I should get headaches because of stress.

12. My inner self does not believe that I should be addicted to any chemical medication to relieve pain.

13. My inner self does not believe that I have to use pain medication to eliminate my pain.

14. My inner self does not believe that I should want to use pain medication to relieve my pain.

15. My inner self does not believe that I should desire or crave any pain medication for any reason.

16. My inner self can imagine me being completely free of all pain.

17. I am able to imagine myself completely free of all pain.

My Inner Self's Character

TRANSFORMING MY INNER SELF

1. My inner self always thinks positively.

2. My inner self always feels positive.

3. My inner self's spirit is always positive.

4. My inner self's spirit is always happy.

5. My inner self is never emotionless for any reason.

6. My inner self never feels unmoved or apathetic for any reason.

7. My inner self is always reliable.

8. My inner self is always consistent.

9. My inner self can overcome all obstacles.

10. My inner self is never passive for any reason.

11. My inner self never feels as if it is running out of time.

12. My inner self never feels unfulfilled for any reason.

13. My inner self never feels as if it is incapable of doing anything, for any reason.

14. My inner self always feels animated.

15. My inner self never feels bored for any reason.

16. My inner self never feels out of control.

17. My inner self never feels dissatisfied for any reason.

18. My inner self never envies anyone for any reason.

19. My inner self is always resourceful.

20. My inner self is always thankful and appreciative.

21. My inner self never feels indifferent for any reason.

22. My inner self will never become cynical for any reason.

23. My inner self never has a problem apologizing for any reason.

24. My inner self is never intolerant for any reason.

25. My inner self's perceptions of things are always positive.

26. My inner self never has a negative perspective for any reason.

27. My inner self does not have a problem saying "no" when appropriate.

28. My inner self is never negatively affected when "no" has to be said.

29. My inner self does not have a problem saying "yes" when appropriate.

30. My inner self does not have a problem compromising when necessary.

31. My inner self does not always act defensively in a negative way.

32. My inner self is honest.

33. My inner self will never feel trapped or imprisoned for any reason.

34. My inner self will never feel as if it is not alive.

35. My inner self is certain about all things.

36. My inner self is happy being itself.

37. My inner self does all things effortlessly.

38. My inner self is always able to tolerate any type of personality.

39. My inner self never feels uncomfortable in any situation.

40. My inner self is always disciplined.

41. My inner self believes in being efficient and organized.

42. My inner self is always efficient and organized.

43. My inner self never feels inferior to anyone for any reason.

44. My inner self cannot be provoked for any reason.

45. My inner self is uninhibited.

46. My inner self will never be self-destructive for any reason.

47. My inner self will never be divisive for any reason.

48. My inner self is never insecure.

49. My inner self can never be pressured to do things that it feels is not right.

50. My inner self always has a good heart that is filled with love and joy.

51. My inner self is always trustworthy.

52. My inner self is never deceitful for any reason.

53. My inner self is never discouraged about anything for any reason.

54. My inner self will never be closed-minded for any reason.

55. My inner self is always open-minded.

56. My inner self never makes excuses for any reason.

57. My inner self is never disrespectful for any reason.

58. My inner self does not have any limitations.

59. My inner self has solutions to all problems.

60. My inner self is emotionally sound and balanced.

61. My inner self is adaptable.

62. My inner self will never be stubborn in a negative way for any reason.

63. My inner self will never lose interest in all things for any reason.

64. My inner self is strong enough to cope with any situation that arises.

65. My inner self is never jealous for any reason.

66. My inner self is never impatient for any reason.

67. My inner self does not believe in arguing for the sake of arguing.

68. My inner self is not argumentative.

69. My inner self never argues in a negative way for any reason.

70. My inner self does not have any harmful or unwanted desires or needs.

71. My inner self is never mean, selfish or self-centered.

72. My inner self is not reclusive.

73. My inner self is always strong.

74. My inner self is never negative.

75. My inner self never feels or thinks negatively for any reason.

76. My inner self is not hateful.

77. My inners self is not vindictive.

78. My inner self is never rude.

79. My inner self is always persistent.

80. My inner self never has difficulties agreeing for any reason.

81. My inner self never has difficulties disagreeing for any reason.

82. My inner self is never bossy for any reason.

83. My inner self is always dependable.

84. My inner self is always good.

85. My inner self is never indecisive for any reason.

86. My inner self is calm.

87. My inner self never becomes tired for any reason.

88. My inner self is never mean for any reason.

89. My inner self is always open to ideas that are contrary to the way that it is accustomed to thinking.

90. My inner self never has a problem with asking for help for any reason.

91. My inner self is never attracted to anything or anyone that is negative.

92. My inner self is able to recover quickly from anything.

93. My inner self never has a problem admitting mistakes for any reason.

94. My inner self is free of all prejudices and biases.

95. My inner self does not believe in being discriminatory or prejudiced for any reason.

96. My inner self is not violent.

97. My inner self is never destructive for any reason.

98. My inner self never wants to quit or give up unless it is absolutely certain that it should.

99. My inner self is always highly motivated to correct promptly any problems that arise.

100. My inner self is never judgmental for any reason.

101. My inner self will never self-destruct for any reason.

102. My inner self is never lazy.

103. My inner self is never inflexible for any reason.

104. My inner self never complains about things that need to be done for any reason.

105. My inner self's mind is never overactive.

106. My inner self is affectionate.

107. My inner self never has a problem admitting when it is wrong.

108. My inner self will never work against me for any reason.

109. My inner self always remains strong, even under the worst of circumstances.

110. My inner self is never interested in anything evil or violent for any reason.

111. My inner self is always able to agree or disagree with anyone.

112. My inner self is never impolite for any reason.

113. My inner self never lacks courage to do what needs to be done for any reason.

114. My inner self is never without integrity.

115. My inner self always agrees with what I am doing as long as it is positive and in my best interest.

116. My inner self is always efficient and organized, never disorganized for any reason.

117. My inner self never has a problem accepting advice for any reason.

118. My inner self is always resilient.

119. My inner self is not cold or callous.

120. My inner self is never insensitive or uncaring.

121. My inner self will never be evil or sinister for any reason.

122. My inner self is always personable.

123. My inner self is always positive, strong and optimistic.

Affects Upon My Inner Self

OPTIMIZING THE WAY EVENTS AND CIRCUMSTANCES AFFECT MY INNER SELF

1. My inner self is not negatively affected by unpleasant memories for any reason.

2. My inner self is not negatively affected by other people's problems.

3. I do not believe that my inner self should be negatively affected by other people's problems for any reason.

4. My inner self believes that I should always be compassionate and caring, and willing to help whenever necessary.

5. My inner self does not believe that other people's opinion of me should ever affect me in a negative way.

6. Other people's opinions never have a negative effect on my inner self for any reason.

7. My inner self is not negatively affected by unfavorable circumstances for any reason.

8. I do not believe that my inner self should be negatively affected by anything that happened in the past, that is happening now, or that may happen in the future.

9. Any unfulfilled desires, wishes, prayers or dreams never negatively affect my inner self.

10. My inner self is not negatively affected by anything, for any reason.

11. My inner self is never negatively affected emotionally for any reason.

12. My inner self is never negatively affected mentally for any reason.

13. My inner self is never negatively affected spiritually for any reason.

14. My inner self does not believe that other people's thoughts, feelings, emotions, words or actions should affect me in a negative way, for any reason.

15. My inner self is never negatively affected when things go wrong.

16. Neither my thoughts nor my imagination will have a negative effect on my inner self.

17. My inner self is never affected when someone says "no".

18. My inner self is never negatively affected by negative thoughts or images for any reason.

19. My inner self's mood is never negatively affected by other people's mood for any reason.

20. My inner self is never affected by negative people for any reason.

21. My inner self is not affected if things do not go according to plan.

22. My inner self is not affected if it does not get what it wants.

23. My inner self is never negatively affected if it is unable to do what it wants to do.

24. My inner self is not negatively affected by women for any reason.

25. My inner self is not negatively affected by men for any reason.

26. My inner self is not negatively affected by children for any reason.

27. My inner self is not negatively affected by anyone for any reason.

28. My inner self is never affected by anything negative for any reason.

29. My inner self is not negatively affected by violent or negative movies or television shows.

30. My inner self is not negatively affected by violent or negative games.

31. My inner self is not negatively affected by violent or negative music.

32. Violent or negative things experienced in the past do not negatively affect my inner self.

33. My inner self's mood is never negatively affected for any reason.

34. My inner self's attitude is never negatively affected for any reason.

35. My inner self is never negatively changed by anyone or anything for any reason.

Weight Management

AIDING WEIGHT LOSS AND ELIMINATING FOOD CRAVINGS

1. My inner self does not think that I should eat when I am not hungry.

2. My inner self does not believe I should be overweight for any reason.

3. My inner self does not believe that I should not care about my weight for any reason.

4. My inner self believes that I should be motivated to lose weight and to obtain an ideal body weight.

5. My inner self believes that I should always be motivated to lose all unwanted weight.

6. My inner self wants me to lose weight.

7. My inner self wants me to eliminate unhealthy foods from my diet.

8. My inner self never craves unhealthy foods for any reason.

9. My inner self does not believe that I should ever crave unhealthy foods.

10. My inner self does not believe that I should ever miss eating any food or drinking any beverage.

11. My inner self has the discipline and the willpower to lose weight.

12. My inner self believes that I should always have the discipline and the willpower to lose weight.

13. My inner self always has the willpower to resist eating or drinking any food or beverage.

14. My inner self does not believe that I should ever eat because of stress.

15. My inner self will never suffer while I am losing weight.

16. My inner self does not believe that I should ever suffer while losing weight.

17. My inner self does not believe that I should ever suffer because I stopped eating any food or stopped drinking any liquid.

18. My inner self wants me to exercise in moderation and consistently.

19. My inner self feels motivated to exercise.

20. My inner self feels motivated to lose weight.

21. My inner self is enthusiastic about losing weight and becoming more physically active.

22. My inner self believes that I should only desire healthy foods.

23. My inner self never craves any foods for any reason.

24. My inner self no longer desires or craves sweets.

25. My inner self no longer desires or craves salt or salty foods.

26. My inner self no longer desires or craves fried foods.

27. My inner self no longer desires or craves cookies, cakes, pies or donuts.

28. My inner self no longer desires or craves potato chips.

29. My inner self no longer desires or craves French fries.

30. My inner self no longer desires or craves ice cream.

31. My inner self no longer desires or craves chocolate.

32. My inner self no longer desires or craves candy.

33. My inner self no longer desires or craves hamburgers.

34. My inner self no longer desires or craves hot dogs.

35. My inner self no longer desires or craves coffee.

36. My inner self does not believe that I should ever crave the above-mentioned foods.

37. My inner self does not want to eat potato chips.

38. My inner self does not want to eat ice cream.

39. My inner self does not want to eat French fries.

40. My inner self does not want to eat chocolate.

41. My inner self does not want to eat candy.

42. My inner self does not want to eat hamburgers.

43. My inner self does not want to eat hot dogs.

44. My inner self does not want to eat sweets.

45. My inner self does not want to eat salty foods.

46. My inner self does not want to eat cookies, cakes, pies or donuts.

47. My inner self does not believe that I should want to eat any of the above-mentioned foods.

48. My inner self does not believe that I should ever miss eating any foods that I eliminated from my diet.

49. My inner self is all right with me missing a meal or decreasing my calorie intake.

50. My inner self believes that I should remain motivated until I reach my desired weight and I should stay motivated to maintain that weight.

51. My inner self believes that I am able to eat less and still feel satisfied.

52. My inner self does not believe that I should consume excessive amounts of food or beverages for any reason.

53. My inner self is highly motivated and determined to lose the number of pounds necessary to reach my weight loss goal.

54. My inner self does not believe that I should ever eat until I am stuffed for any reasons.

55. It is important to my inner self that I lose weight.

56. My inner self does not believe that I should ever make excuses for not losing weight.

Conclusion

Dear Reader,

I WOULD LIKE TO THANK YOU for purchasing my book and using the affirmations. I am confident that, if you used them as instructed, you have benefited immensely. Feel free to use the affirmations as often as you like. I personally read some of the affirmations daily. If you know of someone who could benefit from the book, please spread the word. In the future, I plan to write other books that explore topics not covered in this present work. If you have any recommendations or suggestions of other topics that can be included in future writings, feel free to use either of the contact means provided below.

I look forward to your feedback, comments and testimonials.

Kindest regards,
Sheldon T. Ceaser, M.D.

Website: DoctorCeaser.com
Email: STCeasermd@aol.com
Office: Sheldon T. Ceaser, M.D.
231 E. 75th St
Chicago, Illinois 60619

CPSIA information can be obtained at www.ICGtesting.com
Printed in the USA
LVOW060121190613

339216LV00003B/7/P